40 DAYS

OF

LIGHT

DAN SARDINAS

ISBN 9798332251177
☐

<u>DEDICATION</u>

This book is dedicated to my church family at Northwest Baptist Church. Thank you for your love and support. I look forward to many more exciting days together.

ACKNOWLEDGEMENTS

Thank you to Lori Sardinas and Brenda Vann, who edited and proofread this book in 2013.

CONTENTS

ABOUT THIS BOOK

This book was initially written when I became the pastor at Northwest Baptist Church in 2013. It was never made public in print as the first edition was a spiral-bound book we made in-house at the church office. Because of this, the book has been forgotten and lost throughout the years. I desired to bring it back out with the other books I have written so that it might continue to be a blessing to those who read it. It also provides a snapshot of where our church was at the time.

Let me provide some context to this book and why it was written. I had only written one book before this one and wanted to keep writing to disciple those whom the Lord had entrusted to me at NWBC. I was also praying that this book would be the spark of something new in our church. This is why I deal with sin, bible reading, evangelism, fellowship, love, and worship. The book was to be read over a 40-day period, beginning on October 13th, 2013, and ending on the 40th day on November 24th, 2013. The ending coincided with Thanksgiving, so the last week was about thankfulness and praise.

It was the beginning of many more books that I wrote for Northwest Baptist Church. I write these books not for fame or fortune (there is none) but for the love of these precious saints. I love them and love being their pastor. Our church has changed much over the years, and God continues to reform us through His Word. The Lord has used these books to help shape us and our beliefs. We continue to give these books out for free to all guests of Northwest Baptist Church.

This edition has changed since its first printing in 2013. It has been revised, expanded, and, in some sections, changed altogether. I guess it's safe to say that eleven years later, I have matured more in my writing and theology. This new edition also contains discussion questions at the end of each chapter, which the first edition did not have. The cover art has also changed. The first edition had a picture of a match depicting light. The meaning of that image was that we were praying that God would strike a match and light us ablaze with truth. He did and continues to do so.

God bless you,

Dan

INTRODUCTION

This devotional book has been written to engage and encourage you. Each day, you will find a scripture to read and my thoughts about that scripture. Please read it only ONE day at a time. Even though it might be tempting to read ahead, take your time and soak in the Word. I am praying for you to be challenged, changed, and inspired. My hope is that this will be a life-changing period for you. Let's burn bright and catch fire during these next 40 Days.

WEEK 1

THE LIGHT
OF HIS GLORY

DAY 1
GOD IS A CONSUMING FIRE

"For the Lord your God is a consuming fire, a jealous God."
(Deuteronomy 4:24)

Read: Deuteronomy 4:15-24

Have you ever pondered the unique aspect of God's jealousy, described as a consuming fire? This depiction of God, not commonly discussed, is how the Bible portrays Him. It's crucial to grasp that this is distinct from our human jealousy and selfish ambition. Our jealousy often arises from self-centeredness and darkness within us, casting a shadow on the world around us. However, God's jealousy is righteous and holy, not sinful nor evil. God can't sin. *"This is the message we have heard from him and proclaim to you, that God is light, and in him is no darkness at all" (1 John 1:5)*. God's jealousy is just because it emanates from the beauty of His Glory. God is pure, holy, righteous, and worthy of all worship. All praise and glory belong solely to Him. When others attempt to rob God of what rightfully belongs to Him, he becomes justly jealous.

What is it that God is jealous of? God is jealous of the renown of His name. Through the inspiration of the Holy Spirit, Moses penned the words to describe what makes God burn with righteous jealousy. In context, Moses was specifically saying this to warn Israel of the foolishness of their idolatry. Israel was an idolatrous people and gave the glory that was due to God to anything and everything. God alone is to be worshipped. To worship anything but God is to rob God of the glory that belongs solely to Him. Therefore, He burns as a consuming fire that is fueled by holy jealousy. This glory rightfully belongs to Him. *"To the King of the ages, immortal, invisible, the only God, be honor and glory forever and ever. Amen." (1 Timothy 1:17)* He alone is worthy and deserving.

Sin corrupts us so that we are born with the desire to be consumed with ourselves. Sin wants us to relish in the glory that we think we deserve. Sin deceives us into thinking we are more important than we truly are in this world. There is even a modern sentiment that teaches that "God needs me." Let's be clear: God did not create you because He was lonely. He did not save you because he "had to." He did not call you to serve Him because He needed you. The complete opposite is true. You need Him!

You and I were created, saved, and called for God's glory. As we embark on these 40 Days, I urge you to shift the spotlight off yourself. I encourage you to burn for what makes God burn with joy. I challenge you to dethrone your so-called glory and redirect that to glorify Him. I'm not asking you to make God the Lord. He already is the Lord and, thus, needs no permission from you and me. This shift in thinking can change your perspective as you repent of your sin. This humility is required but can only come as a gift from the Holy Spirit as it's given by grace to sinners.

You will only experience the true satisfaction that your heart desires when your heart surrenders to the light of a holy and jealous God. May the light of His glory shine so that the darkness of your heart vanishes. Whose light shines brighter? Who deserves more praise? Who created whom? What consumes you today? May the glory of God consume your heart, illuminating your path and transforming your life.

"Thus says the Lord, the King of Israel and his Redeemer, the Lord of hosts: "I am the first and I am the last; besides me there is no god. Who is like me? Let him proclaim it. Let him declare and set it before me, since I appointed an ancient people. Let them declare what is to come, and what will happen. Fear not, nor be afraid; have I not told you from of old and declared it? And you are my witnesses! Is there a God besides me? There is no Rock; I know not any." - Isaiah 44:6-8

DISCUSSION QUESTIONS

1. How does the Bible's depiction of God's jealousy differ from human jealousy?

2. What does it mean when the Bible says that God is a consuming fire? How does this imagery help us understand His nature?

3. What are some modern forms of idolatry that we might struggle with today? How can recognizing God's holy jealousy help us combat these?

4. What currently consumes your heart and mind? How can you allow the glory of God to take precedence over these things?

5. What are some practical ways we can redirect our focus from self-centeredness to glorifying God in our everyday lives?

DAY 2
GOD SITS ON A THRONE

*"In the year that King Uzziah died I saw the Lord **sitting upon a throne**," (Isaiah 6:1)*

Read Isaiah 6:1-13

Our God sits on a throne. This throne differs from a typical place where just any old king can sit. This throne holds more beauty, majesty, and worth than every molecule combined—an infinite number of times. He who sits on this throne is worthy of all the worship in the universe. His power, person, and perfection show that He alone is to be awed and feared. This week, I want to break this passage down and be immersed in its beauty. What Isaiah was witnessing was the glory of God on display. This vision of God that sat in authority humbled him and made him quake with great fear. Why?

It was his people (Judah) who were to be taken captive by a ruthless king. King Nebuchadnezzar was to invade Jerusalem and destroy it by the very hand of God. Israel had been warned repeatedly by God's prophets to repent of their wickedness. However, they did not listen and acted as if they sat on this majestic heavenly throne. Each generation continued to sin and drifted further into the depths of idolatry. That is until the patience of God had expired on that forewarned day. Who is in authority? Who is it that demands obedience? The light of God's glory clearly shows an awesome God. Our God sits on a throne in authority!

Idolatry is simply man's attempt to place someone or something other than God on the throne. You will worship whatever you substitute on this throne. What is it that you worship today? Is it the pursuit of wealth? Is it your reputation? Is it being noticed? Is it having your political party win an election? More than likely, the idol that you worship stares at you in the mirror each morning. We are even prone to take the gifts God has given to us and worship them instead of God. There is nobody innocent of idolatry, for every sin a person can commit is the worship of something other than God.

Isaiah witnessed God, who was in authority, sitting on this magnificent throne. Israel's sin mocked God. Israel had forgotten His commandments. They were His people, but they went astray as sheep foolishly do. On this second day of these forty days, please ask yourself the question that faced Isaiah. "Who sits on the throne?" What have you decided to place in authority instead of the Lord? For many people, it is some material or physical possession. For others, it will take the Holy Spirit to awaken their hearts to show them their idolatry.

I stare at my idol in the mirror every morning. Because of my fallen nature, I worship myself. I have placed myself on the throne of my heart that rightfully belongs to the Lord. How about you? Who or what sits on your throne? Don't be so quick to answer, "the Lord." The answer to that question rests in the fruit of your life. Your actions stem from what you truly believe in your heart. The gospel is the only way to acknowledge, worship, and see God for who He truly is. This is why it's all of grace to believe. God does for us what we cannot do for ourselves. The Light of His Glory shines brightly from His Throne!

DISCUSSION QUESTIONS

1. How does Isaiah's vision of the Lord sitting on a throne in Isaiah 6:1-13 emphasize God's majesty and authority?

2. Why do you think Isaiah was so humbled and fearful upon seeing this vision of God?

3. Why is it important to ask ourselves who or what we place on the throne of our hearts?

4. Reflect on the imagery and messages in Isaiah 6:1-13. How do they deepen your understanding of God's holiness and authority?

5. What changes might you need to make in your life to more fully reflect the reality of God's authority and glory?

DAY 3
GOD IS HIGH AND LIFTED UP

Read Isaiah 6:1-13

In the year that King Uzziah died I saw the Lord sitting upon a throne, **high and lifted up;** *(Isaiah 6:1)*

I have discovered that many do not love the God of the Bible. Instead, many are "in lust" with a god, fashioned upon an eclectic rendering of all they like about him. This belief system has produced shallow, fruitless, and perhaps even false disciples. This kind of god is similar to a Mr. Potato Head. Mr. Potato Head has been a childhood favorite for many children. Children can assemble this toy in any way they like. It is only up to the imagination and the preferences of the child. When we treat God like a Mr. Potato Head, we are guilty of idolatry. This is because we cannot pick and choose what we like or don't like about God. Any version of God that is different from how the Scriptures reveal him is blasphemous. This is precisely what some do, and it's because they fail to see the light of His glory.

Some do this, for example, when it comes to specific attributes of God. Many love to talk about God's love but hate His sovereignty and wrath. These attributes are all true of Him and are in accordance with the Scriptures. God hasn't asked you to play favorites but to submit to His Word. The consequences of idolatry are severe, leading to a shallow understanding of God and a false sense of discipleship. Isaiah saw the Lord's throne "high and lifted up." This must be noticed. God does not just reign on the same level as other kings or men. He is above every king and every person. God's glory is shown by where God reigns! God reigns from eternity in glory. God reigns outside of time and space. God reigns from not just one place but everywhere! God is omnipresent. This means that God is everywhere at the same time. God is not just the King of Heaven; He is the King of the universe. Isaiah also reports, "the train of his robe fills the temple." Just how big is God? Many have a very shallow and limited view of God. Is God just a "buddy" to you? How about the "man upstairs?" These weak descriptions of God are often used without much thought. It is true that because of the gospel, we have become "friends of God." We have become friends with God, not so we can view God differently, but so we can view ourselves differently. The Bible says that we were born an enemy of God (Romans 5:10). The gospel changes our position from enemy to friend. This transformation from being enemies of God to becoming His friends is a testament to His grace and love. We are friends of God because we have been spared, by His grace, from the wrath reserved for His enemies.

Idols are easy. They are not real and are crafted by our imaginations. They are made with our own hands and hearts. They are tangible and easily crafted by our cravings and the longings of our flesh. We bring them down to our level. If you think of God as more of your buddy who is "there for you when you need him," you might be worshipping an idol. If you find God cheering you on more in your awesomeness than His, you might be worshipping an idol. If you treat God more like a genie in a bottle than the King of the universe, you might be an idolater. Is it possible that you have lowered God to be someone with whom you can "hang out?" Have you lost the fact that He is "high and lifted up." To view God in any lesser light than He declares to be is blasphemous. It is idolatrous.

Do we lack a fear of God because we have limited the value & worth of a God who is "high & lifted" up? The fear of God, in a sense of terror, but also in a sense of awe and reverence, is a crucial aspect of our relationship with Him. It reminds us of His sovereignty and our humble position before Him.

The light of his glory shows us that since he is "high and lifted up," I cannot bring him down to my level. I cannot "dumb" God down and only accept the parts I love and ignore the parts I hate or don't understand. He is God, and I'm not. He is high and lifted up, not me.

DISCUSSION QUESTIONS

1. Why is it dangerous to create a version of God that aligns with our preferences and dislikes?

2. What does Isaiah's vision of God's throne "high and lifted up" (Isaiah 6:1) teach us about God's sovereignty and glory?

3. How does treating God as a "buddy" or "genie" diminish His true nature and our relationship with Him?

4. How does a proper fear of God affect our daily lives and decisions?

5. What changes might you need to make in your life to reflect a true understanding of God's majesty and authority?

DAY 4
GOD IS HOLY

And one called to another and said: **"Holy, holy, holy** *is the Lord of hosts; the whole earth is full of his glory!" (Isaiah 6:3)*

The scene becomes even more surreal for Isaiah. The seraphim begins worshipping out loud in front of him. They cry out to the Lord with high adoration. They declared to Isaiah that the Lord is "holy, holy, holy." They also stated that the entire earth is filled with His glory. Fire, smoke, and the shaking of the very foundations of this worship service were moved with the praise of this holy God. This unique and unparalleled scene, where God is thrice holy, is a testament to His transcendence. His holiness is what separates Him from you and me. The seraphim spoke the word "holy" three times, the only attribute listed in the Bible that is repeated thrice. The Bible says that God is love, but never love, love, love. Some have even said that holiness is the crowning attribute to describe God. It means that He is far more transcendent than anything else in existence. There is nobody or anything like our God. He is not just holy; he is holy, holy, holy!

Some have said to me that God must be full of Himself. Why does God demand so much attention? Some others have said, "Why does God seem like He's on one big ego trip?" This only appears true to some because they cannot fathom holiness or God's nature. However, if it helps, let us not forget that God is a Trinity. There is one God revealed in three distinct persons. Throughout all the Scriptures, we see how God honors Himself within this context of the Trinity. All three persons of the Godhead worship and praise one another. The Father glories in the Son (Acts 3:13, John 8:54, John 17:1, 5), the Son glories in the Father (John 17:4, John 12:28, 15:8), and the Spirit glories in the Father and the Son (John 16:14). Within the context of the Trinity, we see a gloriously exalted relationship. God lives in perfect harmony and glory in Himself.

Before, there were seconds, minutes, or years before history could be told or the thoughts in man's mind known. Before any seed sprouted or any bird took flight, before molecules split or joined, before neutrons, electrons, or DNA had a code, before any of that, the Father, Son, and Spirit existed in the Holy Trinity. God created the universe because He is love. God did not create creation because it was good, although it was. God created because He is good.

Since God is holy, holy, holy, then he must be known and worshipped. God not only wants His people to see the glory of His name but also the entirety of creation as well! The prophets speak of how

the world would be filled with God's glory as the seas
are filled with water! God wants every country, town,
city, and province to know His name! This is a
common theme seen at the end of the book of Ezekiel.
As Ezekiel is prophesying against the nations around
Israel, God says the same thing repeatedly. He wants all
nations to know that "I am the Lord." God is serious
about His name. God does not fool with His Glory.
The Light of His Glory shows me that God is Holy.

Do you perceive God as Holy?

*"So I will show my greatness and my holiness and make myself
known in the eyes of many nations. Then they will know that I
am the Lord." (Ezekiel 38:23)*

DISCUSSION QUESTIONS

1. How do you respond to the claim that God seems to be on an "ego trip"? How does the concept of the Trinity provide a different perspective?

2. Reflect on the passages where the Father, Son, and Holy Spirit glorify one another (Acts 3:13, John 8:54, John 17:1, 5, John 12:28, 15:8, John 16:14). How do these passages enhance your understanding of the Trinity?

3. What steps can you take to deepen your reverence for God and align your worship with the vision of His holiness depicted in Isaiah?

4. How does the scene of fire, smoke, and shaking foundations contribute to the understanding of God's holiness and majesty?

5. Why do you think the attribute of holiness is emphasized more than others in the Bible (e.g., "holy, holy, holy" vs. "love, love, love")?

DAY 5
GOD'S GLORY EXPOSES OUR HEARTS

And I said: "Woe is me! For I am lost; for I am a man of unclean lips, and I dwell in the midst of a people of unclean lips; for my eyes have seen the King, the Lord of hosts!" – Isaiah 6:5

The light of God's glory does not just show us God for His beauty. It also enlightens us about our spiritual bankruptcy, devoid of spiritual wealth or righteousness. We will see ourselves as wicked when we fully see God as Holy. Isaiah had this enlightening moment when he encountered the holiness of God. When he observed the light of God's glory, burning bright from God's declared & visible holiness, Isaiah cried out! Isaiah knew that his standing before God was bankrupt. He stated, "Woe is me." This was an expression of deep anguish and sorrow. It was not a phrase that one used for performance but in authenticity. Standing before a Holy, Righteous, and Eternal God, Isaiah realized that he was nothing in comparison. He understood that he had nothing to offer this Holy God that could genuinely satisfy His wrath against his sin. He also confessed that he was lost, unclean, and lived amongst an unholy people. How does Isaiah come to this conclusion? *"For my eyes have seen the King, the Lord of hosts!"* Standing before God, gazing upon His beauty, and leaving unchanged is impossible. The light of God's glory exposes our dark, ugly, and depraved hearts.

Isaiah did not come to this conclusion because he was comparing himself to his countrymen. He came to this conclusion because He saw the light of God's glory, and it melted his sinful pride. Who are you comparing yourself with today? Many of us love to compare ourselves to other people. Every human being you will ever compare yourself with is also a sinner. When you compare yourself to another person (for the worse or the better), you ultimately set yourself up for failure. The only real change happens when you compare yourself to God. Transforming power comes through an awareness of our spiritual indebtedness compared to His magnificent beauty. This is why the gospel is an essential aspect of our lives. Because of God's kindness, we are led to repentance. The gospel allows me to partake in the glorious exchange! I received His righteousness, and He took my sin. Repentance is not a passive action but a command to be obeyed. We are responsible for recognizing our sin, confessing it, and turning away from it, knowing that God's grace is what empowers it.

Isaiah saw God not only in holiness but also as authoritative. He saw God as "the King." Isaiah knew that this God was worthy of all his obedience. Isaiah knew to be in His presence was to see himself in submission to this Holy God. Is God truly your King? Do you think that you are in control of your life? Recognizing God's authority is not a sign of weakness but of humility and worship. It is a reminder that we are not the masters of our own lives, but that we are under the loving and just rule of our Heavenly King. What sin do you have that needs to be confessed and repented? You will only see it as the light of His Glory shines down on you and exposes you for who you are. This might sound like a painful exercise; however, it is the most appropriate response in love to a thrice Holy God. Isaiah saw his sin; do you see yours? What do you do with your sin? Will you repent, considering the magnificence of this glorious God?

DISCUSSION QUESTIONS

1. How does Isaiah's encounter with God's holiness in Isaiah 6 reveal his own spiritual bankruptcy?

2. What does Isaiah's "Woe is me" cry teach us about authentic repentance and recognizing our sinfulness?

3. Why is comparing ourselves to others spiritually dangerous and ultimately unproductive? How does comparing ourselves to God's holiness instead lead to true spiritual transformation?

4. Reflect on a time when you felt the weight of your own sinfulness in the light of God's holiness. How did that experience impact you?

5. What are some specific sins in your life that you need to confess and repent of? How can you seek God's grace to overcome them?

DAY 6
GOD'S GLORY IS WHY I'M SAVED

"Then one of the seraphim flew to me, having in his hand a burning coal that he had taken with tongs from the altar. And he touched my mouth and said: "Behold, this has touched your lips; your guilt is taken away, and your sin atoned for." (Isaiah 6:6-7)

Isaiah repented of his sins because of the weight and beauty of God's glory. He saw the beauty of God contrasted against the horror of his sins and his people. We know that repentance brings glory to God. Jesus tells us that there is joy for even one sinner who repents. It did not end there for Isaiah. God's glory also led to the forgiveness and atonement of Isaiah's sins. When someone comes to repentance and turns from their sin to God, it is always for God's glory. The very reason God saves people is for His glory. What an astounding thought. It gives God immeasurable pleasure and joy to save those who believe. God is the only one who can take the glory for saving anybody because salvation is strictly from His grace. Salvation is planned, delivered, and accomplished through and for God.

God did not save you for your benefit. Although, we benefit significantly from being saved from His wrath. God saved us because it gives Him ultimate joy. Jesus did not come in the flesh, perfectly obey the law, and die your death so that you will be honored. When Jesus was enduring the wrath of God for our sins, he was not thinking about you "above all." He was dying for God's Glory. He was absorbing the full wrath, weight, and judgment for sin so that the wrath of God would be perfectly satisfied. He creates, calls, and saves "for his name's sake." When you realize how awesome, majestic, glorious, and bright this God is, you can't help but respond with a "Woe is me." Read these verses and see God's motivation for why He saves and forgives.

We are saved because He loves to display the light of his glory to hell-bound sinners.

"For my name's sake I defer my anger, for the sake of my praise I restrain it for you, that I may not cut you off. Behold, I have refined you, but not as silver; I have tried you in the furnace of affliction. For my own sake, for my own sake, I do it, for how should my name be profaned? My glory I will not give to another. Isaiah 48:9-11

I am writing to you, little children, because your sins are forgiven for his name's sake. - 1 John 2:12

Thus says the Lord God, It is not for your sake, O house of Israel, that I am about to act, but for the sake of my holy name .

. . And I will vindicate the holiness of my great name . . .. And the nations will know that I am the Lord. (Ezekiel 36:22-23; cf. v. 32)

I, I am he who blots out your transgressions for my own sake, and I will not remember your sins. (Isaiah 43:25)

For your own name's sake, O Lord, pardon my guilt, for it is great. (Psalm 25:11)

The light of his glory saves you for His own pleasure and for your good!

DISCUSSION QUESTIONS

1. According to the passages mentioned, why does God save people? Have you ever considered why God saved you? If so, what did you think his ultimate purpose was?

2. How does the concept that God saves for His own glory impact your understanding of salvation? Can man then contribute anything to it?

3. What does it mean that Jesus absorbed the wrath of God to satisfy His justice and bring glory to God?

4. How can you apply the truth of God's glory in salvation to your personal evangelism and witness to others?

5. How does embracing God's sovereignty in salvation and forgiveness bring comfort and assurance to believers?

DAY 7
GOD'S GLORY CALLS ME INTO SERVICE

And I heard the voice of the Lord saying, "Whom shall I send, and who will go for us?" Then I said, "Here I am! Send me." –
Isaiah 6:8

Isaiah could not leave God's presence without a robust passion to serve God! Having a clear picture of God's holiness and glory will propel us to serve Him passionately! This is what happened in Isaiah as God asked a pointed question. Isaiah did not hesitate to respond to God's question. How could he answer any other way after seeing what he just saw? He emphatically declared his presence and availability. *"Here I am! Send me."* How else could Isaiah respond? If he believed what he saw, there was no other choice. He saw the LORD as the KING and in AUTHORITY.

We must respond to the King's call, for He is worthy of our obedience. As you read this, you may not feel the same as Isaiah. But the question for you should shift to "How do you see God?" Do you see Him as Isaiah did, sitting on a throne, high and lifted up, filling the temple, HOLY, HOLY, HOLY, righteous, glorious, worthy of all the universe's praise? Or have you placed the spotlight on yourself, seeing yourself as the hero of the story? The Bible does not tell us of any heroes; instead, it proclaims the triumph of a faithful, holy, and loving God who chose, empowered, and redeemed men and women for the sake of His name and the renown of His Glory.

Perhaps you are not willing to respond to God as Isaiah did because you see Him as a means to an end. Do you only want to worship God for the "blessings" He has given you? Do you only sing His praises when things are going your way? To seek the blessing more than the Blesser is idolatry. But when we live for the praise of His name, our reason for living becomes much more apparent. Israel could not comprehend this truth. Almost the entire Old Testament is the story of how unfaithful God's people were to His name. They repeatedly failed God by serving and worshiping other gods. They allowed the influence of the surrounding pagan nations to infiltrate and deceive them. Evil kings who loved the gods of the land more than the God of their Fathers led Israel astray.

Once the praise of God begins, it will forever change you! Look around you! You are not the only one or thing worshipping. The heavens declare the glory of God! This God is to be praised in all that He does and for all who He is. This God has no equal.

How do you respond to Him? It all depends on how you see the "Light of His Glory."

If you see God in his holiness, you will also respond as Isaiah did. "Here I am! Send me." So, how will you respond? If you are not moved to an answer, perhaps you have a vision problem. Read Isaiah 6 repeatedly and pray that God gives you such a high and majestic burden for God's glory. There is no other way to respond to this God but with obedience and service.

DISCUSSION QUESTIONS

1. Why did Isaiah respond with such enthusiasm and immediacy to God's call? ("Here I am! Send me.")

2. What factors might influence our perception of God as holy and glorious versus seeing Him as a means to an end?

3. What are some signs that we might be worshiping the blessings more than the Blesser? How can we correct this mindset?

4. How can we cultivate a heart of obedience and readiness to serve like Isaiah?

5. What are your motives for serving God? Are they aligned with bringing glory to His name, or are they more self-centered?

☐

WEEK 2

THE LIGHT OF HIS WORD

DAY 8
THE MEMORY OF THE WORD IN ME

How can a young man keep his way pure? By guarding it according to your word. With my whole heart I seek you; let me not wander from your commandments! I have stored up your word in my heart, that I might not sin against you. Blessed are you, O Lord; teach me your statutes! With my lips I declare all the rules of your mouth. In the way of your testimonies I delight as much as in all riches. I will meditate on your precepts and fix my eyes on your ways. I will delight in your statutes; I will not forget your word. (Psalm 119:9-16)

This week, we will change our focus and look intently at another biblical light. The Bible declares itself to be illuminating. When we read the Bible, we are reading the very words of God. These words are alive and powerful. Have you ever stopped and meditated on that fantastic truth? The way God created the universe was by speaking. We hold in our hands the same power that creates life. Moses tells us everything was dark until God declared, "Let there be light." Not only is light created by the very words that God spoke, but it also provides light into what God wants us to know.

Psalm 119 is devoted entirely to the Psalmist's love of God and His word. In verse 9, he asks a rhetorical question. This question is about the desire of those to live according to the ways of God. According to the Psalmist, the answer to this question is to guard everything against Scripture. How is this accomplished? Doesn't it seem like a daunting task? The Psalmist desires to use God's words as a shield against sin. He has positioned the word of God as his defense even before temptation arises.

Yes, we will stumble, but we must be armed with God's word to face temptation. The Psalmist' stored up your word in my heart.' The concept of 'stored' here implies that he concealed or hoarded the word. He was prepared for defense and offense. What was he ready to confront? It was his self, his sinful nature. The Psalmist understood the necessity of memorizing God's word so "that he might not sin." Did you know that our greatest adversary is often ourselves?

Nobody has failed you more than you have failed yourself. No one has lied to you more than you have lied to yourself. Our hearts are dark and lead us astray often. We need the light of God's illuminating word in our hearts to know the truth. We all need to hide the Word in our hearts. How are you guarding your heart (defense) today? How are you "storing" God's word deep within? (offense).

When Jesus was in the wilderness for 40 days, he used Scripture to fend off the temptations of Satan. If Jesus needed to memorize the word, how much more should we?

DISCUSSION QUESTIONS

1. What does it mean that God's words are alive and powerful? How have you experienced this in your own life?

2. Reflect on the creation story where God spoke light into existence. How does this reinforce the power and authority of God's words? How can this understanding of God's creative power through His word shape our approach to reading the Bible?

3. How does guarding our lives according to Scripture protect us from sin and temptation?

4. How can we use Scripture as both a defense and offense against temptation in our lives?

5. How can we maintain a long-term commitment to reading, memorizing, and meditating on Scripture? What habits or routines can help us integrate the Bible more fully into our daily lives?

DAY 9
THE LIFE OF THE WORD IN ME

My soul clings to the dust; give me life according to your word! When I told of my ways, you answered me; teach me your statutes! Make me understand the way of your precepts, and I will meditate on your wondrous works. My soul melts away for sorrow; strengthen me according to your word! Put false ways far from me and graciously teach me your law! I have chosen the way of faithfulness; I set your rules before me. I cling to your testimonies, O Lord; let me not be put to shame! I will run in the way of your commandments when you enlarge my heart! (Psalm 119:25-32)

We attempt to satisfy our longings with things that keep us longing. We live to give ourselves life with that which has no life. This is precisely what the Psalmist says in verse 25. He admits that he is prone to crave the "dust." Dust? Who would ever crave dust? Indoor dust mainly comprises of dead skin cells and microscopic organisms (mites). Nothing is satisfying or enriching about dust. This amplifies the ridiculousness of this statement. He says that the natural inclination of his heart is to be disappointed in things that do not matter. In other words, you and I crave dust. We seek to get life from that which has no life. True spiritual life can only be found in the Word of God.

Several years ago, there was a documentary called Supersize Me. It was a 30-day video journey of a man who decided to eat nothing but McDonald's. Yes, McDonald's for breakfast, lunch, and dinner. As you can imagine, he was not physically well at the end of the 30 days. He was sick and had gained weight. A doctor who had recorded any changes in his health said the changes were astounding. This man wanted to prove a point, and he did just that. What's the point? You cannot get life from that which has no life. McDonald's food is not made up of all-natural and healthy ingredients. Yes, eating the food fulfilled a caloric requirement, but at the expense of his health.

The problem for many is that we fill our spiritual hunger with things that produce no life. This is because we crave dust. Who would want to eat dust? But we do precisely this when we try to be satisfied in our sin and the temporal things of this world. When we do this, our hunger for the Word is replaced with things that make us spiritually sick. If you "eat" that kind of food every day, you will eventually pay the consequences. Many Christians wonder why their spiritual lives are "dry" and not what they once were. They ask why do I feel as if God is far away? Why do I feel no joy? It's because they have eaten nothing healthy of late. They have filled their spirits with junk, and the effects will show the evidence over time. Repent and read the Word!

It's probably no secret that many Christians are addicted to their smartphones and social media. Many spend hours consuming mindless garbage and wonder why they are so spiritually inept. It's because you are neglecting time with God and are starving yourself spiritually. It's time to put down our smartphones and spend more time in the Word. It's time to turn off the TV and meditate on God and his truth. It's time to pray and let the Word it marinate deep within our hearts. Can you imagine someone turning down a delicious meal for a plate of dust? The dust will not satisfy! Come to the table and feast on God's word. The light of the Word gives life!

DISCUSSION QUESTIONS

1. What does the Psalmist mean when he says he craves "dust"? How does this metaphor apply to our spiritual lives?

2. What are some modern examples of "dust" that people crave and rely on for satisfaction?

3. Reflect on your own life. Are there areas where you have been seeking satisfaction in things that cannot provide true life? How can you identify and remove these "dust" cravings from your life?

4. What does it mean to "feast" on God's Word? How can we make this a delightful and enriching experience?

5. What are some signs that someone is spiritually malnourished?

DAY 10
THE LOVE OF THE WORD IN ME

The Lord is my portion; I promise to keep your words. I entreat your favor with all my heart; be gracious to me according to your promise. When I think on my ways, I turn my feet to your testimonies; I hasten and do not delay to keep your commandments. Though the cords of the wicked ensnare me, I do not forget your law. At midnight I rise to praise you, because of your righteous rules. I am a companion of all who fear you, of those who keep your precepts. The earth, O Lord, is full of your steadfast love; teach me your statutes! – Psalm 119:57-64

Do you remember your emotions when you first realized your spouse was "the one?" Before I worked up enough nerve to ask my wife, Lori, on a date, I longed to see and talk with her. I met her in the very first college class I attended. The class was one of my least favorite subjects, but it instantly became a hit with me. Why? It was because Lori was in this class. This was the one hour I knew I could see Lori. I didn't even know that she knew I existed. However, I knew full well that she was there and thought she was beautiful. I loved to hear her voice answer the questions in class. It wasn't until a year later that I asked her on a date, and life has never been the same.

During the summer break of 1996, Lori and I did not see each other for three months. She lived in Maine, and I lived in New Jersey. I would check my mailbox daily to see if the mailman had delivered any mail from her. I wanted to read what she had to say. I tried to smell the paper (she sprayed her perfume on each note), which reminded me of her while I read it. I could not get enough of it. You didn't have to force me to read her letters. I wanted to read it! I loved her and wanted to treasure every Word she had written. I still have the notes that she wrote to me during these days. These are sweet memories. She captured my heart and showed me her sweet spirit; I was a goner.

You see an even greater love and desire for God and His Word as you read the Psalms. This is incredibly convicting to me. How much do I love God's Word? Do I just read it out of duty? Or do I deeply desire it? Read again how the Psalmist describes his response to the Word. His response does not come from obligation but from passionate obedience. He "turns his feet" to obey God. He does not "delay to keep your commandments." Through the tough times when his enemies are trapping him," I do not forget your law." He even wakes up in the middle of the night to praise God for "your righteous rules." Reading this response to the Word is convicting for me. How much do I desire God's Word? How much do I love it? Do I treasure every Word written? Do I long to reread it the next day?

Many read the Bible out of duty, hoping to "love" it but struggle. The problem lies within our hearts. We are trying to shine our light of "wisdom and understanding" on the Bible, hoping that something will stick. However, this love of the Word comes from outside of us. This is God's work within us. His Spirit produces a love for His Word in every true believer. It's not a self-manufactured or manipulated kind of love. He changes our hearts and puts the love for Him and His Word within us. Just as I did not have to be forced to read Lori's letters because I loved her, so should we desire greatly to read God's Word because we love Him.

May the gospel produce a love for God and His Word in your heart. If you lack desire or love for His Word, it may be time to check your heart. The light of the Word produces a love for me for me to treasure it.

DISCUSSION QUESTIONS

1. What emotions or desires do you experience when you read the Bible? Do you find yourself reading out of duty or genuine love?

2. What specific actions did the Psalmist take to show his love for God's Word (e.g., turning his feet, not delaying to keep commandments, remembering God's law in tough times)?

3. How can we identify if our hearts are not aligned with a true love for God's Word? What steps can we take to align our hearts with the love for God and His Word that the Psalmist describes?

4. How has reading God's Word transformed your life in the past? Can you share a specific example? In what ways can a consistent and passionate engagement with Scripture continue to transform you?

5. How does my experience of longing for Lori's letters parallel our longing for God's presence through His Word? Do you have something like that you can use as an example?

DAY 11
THE PROMISE OF THE WORD IN ME

"My soul longs for your salvation; I hope in your word. My eyes long for your promise; I ask, "When will you comfort me?" For I have become like a wineskin in the smoke, yet I have not forgotten your statutes. How long must your servant endure? When will you judge those who persecute me? The insolent have dug pitfalls for me; they do not live according to your law. All your commandments are sure; they persecute me with falsehood; help me! They have almost made an end of me on earth, but I have not forsaken your precepts. In your steadfast love give me life, that I may keep the testimonies of your mouth." – Psalm 119:81-88

When your life falls apart, what brings you hope? Some run to sports teams, the stock market, and political systems for hope. But let's be honest, these are all fleeting and often disappointing sources of hope. I'm so glad that my hope in life is not in the New York Yankees. The Yankees, the world's most accomplished sports franchise, has had much to celebrate over the years. They own and hold the record of 27 world championships. They have been in existence since 1901, spanning over 100 years of competitive play. Although they have won a record 27 times, it also means they have not been successful in nearly 100 of those years. The Yankees have left their fans disappointed many times.

The stock market has crashed numerous times over the years. Some have made fortunes through the market, but others have lost more. The stock market changes every day, and tomorrow is not guaranteed. You may earn a few dollars or lose thousands. This is not a system in which to hope, either. Politics also poses a nightmare for real hope. What happens when your political party wins or doesn't? What happens when policies and laws that you believe are unconstitutional are established? I've seen many depressed and discouraged Christians who act as if their hope is dependent on who lives in the White House. The disappointment in political outcomes can be overwhelming, and it's a stark reminder of the futility of placing our hope in such systems. I am so thankful that, as a Christian, my hope is in a much greater Kingdom.

The Psalmist knew that his hope and deliverance was in a much greater Rescuer. The Psalmist longed for the promises of God. He did not "forget" God's statutes even during desperation and challenging times. His enemies were winning, and all hope had seemed lost, but he was reminded of one thing that mattered. He was reminded of God's steadfast love. His unwavering faith in God's promises, even in the face of overwhelming challenges, is a powerful testament to the strength that faith can bring. The Bible tells us of a Faithful God who loves His people and gives them abundant promise and hope. A daily reminder of the gospel is a necessity for each believer.

How often do you remember the promises that God has for you? Every day, we are surrounded by people who disappoint and let us down. However, we can be confident that our God is Sovereign on the throne. The Psalmist knew that God had promised to save him. By remembering this promise, he could endure the darkest days. If you are not reading the Bible daily, how can you know what God has promised? May you start reading His word daily, and may His Spirit create a longing for God within your soul. What is your plan to make sure you read and are reminded of God's promises daily? Get in the Word.

The light of His Word brings me hope and a promise.

DISCUSSION QUESTIONS

1. When life falls apart, what are some common places people turn to for hope, and why are these often disappointing?

2. Reflect on your own life. What sources of hope have you turned to in difficult times, and how reliable were they?

3. How does placing our hope in God's Kingdom differ from placing our hope in worldly systems?

4. How often do you remember and reflect on the promises that God has for you? In what ways can a daily reminder of the gospel strengthen your faith and hope?

5. What is your current plan or routine for reading the Bible daily? How effective has it been? What changes or improvements can you make to ensure that you are consistently reminded of God's promises?

DAY 12
THE BENEFITS OF THE WORD IN ME

Oh how I love your law! It is my meditation all the day. Your commandment makes me wiser than my enemies, for it is ever with me. I have more understanding than all my teachers, for your testimonies are my meditation. I understand more than the aged, for I keep your precepts. I hold back my feet from every evil way, in order to keep your word. I do not turn aside from your rules, for you have taught me. How sweet are your words to my taste, sweeter than honey to my mouth! Through your precepts I get understanding; therefore I hate every false way. – Psalm 119:97-104

Have you ever had a cram session? I did this occasionally in college when I ran out of time to study. It also happened when I got to class and was informed by my classmates that a quiz was coming that I had not anticipated. I would take out my notes or the textbook and scan the material. I wanted to absorb as much information as possible to answer the quiz or test questions. Sometimes, this worked in my favor, and at other times, this hurt me. Regardless of the result of the test or quiz that day, the fact is that I no longer remember what I crammed into my head. The cramming had served its immediate purpose. It was to get a grade on a quiz. It did not benefit my learning because I had purposed to use the information in an unintended way.

I believe many people read the Bible this way. They do not read it for long-term life transformation, but they use it as a cram session to get what is needed at that moment. The Psalmist said God's law was his "meditation all the day." The Word used here for meditation implies a deep and thorough study. It is a study that causes a deep reflection within the reader. This reflection can be remembered and utilized throughout the day. He did this out of a motivation of love. He loved the law of God! He knew that it made him wiser than his enemies and more learned than that of his elders. He knew how to live because he could recall what he read and apply it to his life accordingly.

We need to intently read and use every Word and root it deep within our hearts. We need to let these words marinate within our souls. When meat marinates in its seasoning, it soaks up the flavor and juices deep within. The longer the meat sits marinating, the better it tastes! The flavor that permeates the meat is released with every bite and floods our taste buds with epic goodness. Similarly, when we let the words of the Bible marinate within our souls, we experience a deep sense of fulfillment and contentment, knowing that we are nourishing our spiritual lives..

This needs to be our attitude regarding the Word of God. Don't read it as a quick cram session in which you will forget what is said an hour after it is read. Read it and let it marinate deep within you. Ponder over it again and again. Write it down. Memorize it. Engage with it actively. The benefits of the Word within you get better and better over time. These words make us wise to spiritual things as His Holy Spirit teaches. This is what the Psalmist means when he says he "meditates." May the light of God's Word be your meditation so your heart can joy in God!

DISCUSSION QUESTIONS

1. Have you ever had a cram session for a test or quiz? What was the outcome? How does cramming for a test differ from long-term learning and retention?

2. What are the potential pitfalls of using the Bible in a "cram session" manner rather than for long-term spiritual growth?

3. What does it mean when the Psalmist says God's law is his "meditation all the day"? How does deep and thorough study of Scripture differ from quick, superficial reading?

4. Read Psalm 119:97-104. How does this passage highlight the benefits of meditating on God's law? How can these verses inspire you to deepen your commitment to Scripture meditation?

5. How can we actively engage with Scripture throughout the day, beyond our dedicated study time? What habits or routines can help reinforce the practice of meditation on God's Word?

DAY 13
THE LONGING OF THE WORD IN ME

Your testimonies are wonderful; therefore my soul keeps them.
The unfolding of your words gives light; it imparts understanding
to the simple. I open my mouth and pant, because I long for your
commandments. Turn to me and be gracious to me, as is your
way with those who love your name. Keep steady my steps
according to your promise, and let no iniquity get dominion over
me. Redeem me from man's oppression, that I may keep your
precepts. Make your face shine upon your servant, and teach me
your statutes. My eyes shed streams of tears, because people do not
keep your law. — Psalm 119:129-136

Disciples are not just men who followed Jesus
while He lived on earth. Disciples are not people who
have it all together. Every single born-again believer in
Jesus Christ is a disciple. Disciple implies two critical
thoughts: First, a disciple is a follower. We get this idea
immediately when Jesus called His first disciples. They
immediately dropped their nets and followed Him.
They went everywhere that Jesus went. They forsook
their lives, families, and occupations to follow Jesus.

Secondly, disciples are learners. It would not
have been enough for these men to follow Jesus on
earth. They did not just observe, but they learned and
imitated Him. They were learning how to live and how

God's Kingdom worked. Disciples ask a lot of questions. Jesus often taught His disciples by telling them more stories or asking them questions in response to their questions. It was assumed that a disciple was a teachable person.

How teachable are you? Are you willing to unlearn certain things that you have wrong? What if what you believe to be true is taught as wrong in the Bible? What is your response? Does your way win, or does God's? Daily reading God's Word brings truth to our hearts and enlightens us to His ways. Does your worldview line up with the Bible? Or do you interpret the Bible from your worldview? If you are honest, you probably do a little of both without fully realizing it.

The Psalmist knew the only way to learn was to be immersed in God's words. He is declaring that God's words bring "light." Light has a startling relationship with darkness. It repels darkness. If you shine a light into a dark room, you can see where you are going. Without the light, you might stumble and fall or hurt yourself. This is why understanding your identity as a disciple is crucial. We must always yield our will and Spirit to His truth, even though it might be painful.

A teachable spirit quenches a thirsty soul. Psalm 119 convicts me repeatedly. However, I am stunned by the words he uses in verse 131. *"I open my mouth and pant because I long for your commandments."* Wow. If I don't read my Bible today, is my soul left with this same kind of thirst? The honest answer to that question is embarrassing. I don't believe he was saying he was craving a fix, as someone does with their morning coffee. He knew that his soul needed the Word to live! He desired the nourishment and refreshment that the Word brought him. He needed God's light to shine upon his heart to learn more about himself. Always be teachable. Read, learn, and apply God's Word to your life.

Stay thirsty! I pray that the Spirit will cause the Light of the Word to cause a thirst that makes you pant with an undying need for God. Since you are a believer, you are a disciple, after all. Isn't that what disciples do? Yes, they follow and long after their Master! What is the most natural way for a disciple to long for the Master's way? It is to benefit from the light of every word from his mouth!

DISCUSSION QUESTIONS

☐

1. How teachable do you consider yourself to be when it comes to spiritual matters? Are you willing to unlearn certain beliefs if they are shown to be wrong according to the Bible? How do you respond when you encounter a biblical teaching that contradicts your current worldview or beliefs?

2. How does daily reading and studying God's Word help shape your identity as a disciple? What practical steps can you take to ensure that you are consistently engaging with Scripture and allowing it to transform your heart and mind?

3. In Psalm 119:131, the Psalmist expresses a deep longing for God's commandments. How does this kind of thirst for God's Word compare to your own desire for Scripture? What can you learn from the Psalmist's attitude towards God's Word, and how can you cultivate a similar longing in your own life?

4. Do you interpret the Bible through your worldview, or do you allow the Bible to shape your worldview? Give examples of how this has played out in your life.

5. What does it mean to yield your will and spirit to God's truth, even when it is painful? Can you share an

experience where you had to do this? How does a
teachable spirit contribute to your growth as a disciple?

DAY 14
THE PEACE OF THE WORD IN ME

"Princes persecute me without cause, but my heart stands in awe of your words. I rejoice at your word like one who finds great spoil. I hate and abhor falsehood, but I love your law. Seven times a day I praise you for your righteous rules. Great peace have those who love your law; nothing can make them stumble. I hope for your salvation, O Lord, and I do your commandments. My soul keeps your testimonies; I love them exceedingly. I keep your precepts and testimonies, for all my ways are before you."
Psalm 119:161-168

I don't remember where I was or who was with me then. However, I do remember some details very well. An unidentifiable object caught my eye about 75-100 feet before me. I remember the white floor and an empty hallway. It may have been in a mall or an airport. As I approached the object, my heart began to beat with excitement. I began to wish that this was what I had hoped. As I approached closer, I was beginning to realize that my wish was coming true. I stooped over and picked up a twenty-dollar bill off the floor. Twenty dollars?!?! I'm rich! Do you know what I can buy with this? I acted like I had just inherited millions of dollars. I don't even remember what I bought with that money. But I do remember the joy of finding that treasure. But I do remember the joy and peace of finding that treasure. It was as if all my problems had vanquished in a moment. I treated that twenty dollars as the answer I had longed for my entire life.

The Psalmist continues to express his love for the Word in this very long chapter. *"I rejoice at your word like one who finds great spoil."* What a fantastic attitude in beholding the Word of God. Finding truth in the Word for the Psalmist was like an eight-year-old finding a twenty-dollar bill on the floor. At eight years old, I had no idea about the value of money. But I believed that what I found was about to reveal much happiness.. What if we approached the Bible with as much excitement? Do you just read the Bible to "get it done"? Are you going through the motions? Are you finding what you read to be of no value? It may stem from a wrong understanding of the Word's beauty, majesty, and power.

Our God speaks. He spoke the worlds into existence. He speaks to us through His written Word. Do you fully comprehend that? I need to remember. You might forget as well. We hold the greatest treasure in our hands. Why don't you celebrate that you are wealthy today?

DISCUSSION QUESTIONS

☐ 1. Can you recall a time when you found something unexpectedly valuable, similar to me finding the twenty-dollar bill? How did it make you feel?

2. How does this experience help you relate to the joy and excitement the Psalmist feels towards God's Word?

3. How do you currently approach reading the Bible? Do you feel excitement, or does it sometimes feel like a routine task?

4. What changes can you make to approach the Bible with the same joy and anticipation as finding a hidden treasure?

5. How can we overcome spiritual apathy and develop a consistent and meaningful engagement with Scripture?

WEEK 3

THE LIGHT OF THE CITY

DAY 15
A CITY ON A HILL

"You are the light of the world. A city set on a hill cannot be hidden." – Matthew 5:14

There is a question that haunts me. I find myself asking it again and again at various stages of my life and ministry. Sometimes, this question is fueled by a selfish ambition, and other times, it's a genuine desire to glorify God. I'm not embarrassed to confess this because you may also struggle. The question is one of impact. The question I ask is, "Am I making a difference? Can people see God shining through me? Are people noticing me? Or are they noticing the God who is working through me?"

Have you ever been blinded by a light turned on in a dark room? You have no problem noticing the light. Correct? The interesting thing about light is that it doesn't have to "work" to be noticed. The photons that gather to form light are just what they were made to be. They are noticed because their identity is light. They don't have to work harder to be light; they already are. Light has one unmistakable property: it repels darkness. The same is true for Christians.

Understanding our identity is crucial to fulfilling our mission.

The difference we make comes from a proper understanding of identity. If I focus on "shining for God," then it becomes a self-centered quest. If the question develops into God "shining through me," then it's a God-centered vision. Because of the gospel, I have been declared to be the "light of the world." This light does not originate from me, but it comes from God. My life is evidence to a dark world that there is hope. When I understand my role in reaching my community, people are pointed toward God. The difference I make to those around me is an overflow of the gospel's impact within my heart. The only light that shines from my heart is the light that emanates from the glory God receives from a transformed heart. He called me, saved me, and changed me! The difference in me is noticeable because the power of the gospel is creating me to become more like Jesus every day.

Let's return to that room where we found ourselves temporarily blinded. The light has been turned off, and our eyes are forced to adjust to the new darkness. The absence of light quickly becomes evident to all. I began to think through this concept regarding our church. Do the people in our city know that there is a light shining? If our church ceased to exist today, would anyone notice? It is only natural to see that light is missing. God has called us to be a city on a hill! As Jesus said, a city on a hill cannot be hidden because its light can be seen far away. What impact is your light making by God shining through you? Are you turning the "light" on in a dark world? God has called His people to be his "light" in this world as he lights us ablaze with his glory and love to reflect Him. Light makes an impact on darkness. It cannot do anything else because that is its nature.

DISCUSSION QUESTIONS

1. How can you differentiate between a selfish ambition and a genuine desire to glorify God in your quest to make an impact?

2. How does the analogy of light help you understand your identity as a Christian? What does it mean for you to be the "light of the world"? How does this understanding affect your daily life and actions?

3. How does the presence of light naturally repel darkness? How can this be applied to your role as a Christian in the world?

4. How can you keep reminding yourself that the light you shine comes from God and not from your own efforts?

5. How do you feel about God's call to be His light in the world? What excites you about this call, and what challenges do you foresee? How can you prepare yourself spiritually and practically to respond to this call effectively?

DAY 16
A LIGHT ON A STAND

"Nor do people light a lamp and put it under a basket, but on a stand, and it gives light to all in the house." – Matthew 5:15

Light has a unique purpose: to show what lies underneath the cover of darkness. In this verse, Jesus is teaching the necessity of making the light he has given visible. Jesus' point is simple. If you have a light in your home, make it visible so all can see it. Jesus says nobody lights a lamp and hides it under a basket. The lamp is placed on a stand. It is placed in proximity so that all can see it. It is strategically placed where the light can most impact darkness.

This begs us to transform our thinking regarding missional activity. For many, missionary work is just about sending money away so others can do the work. Jesus never taught that. Jesus engaged and trained his disciples to always be near those apart from God. Jesus often ate and spent time with the most unlikely of people. This is not a program that Jesus had as a part of His ministry. This was Jesus' ministry. Jesus said that He came to "seek and save the lost." His mission was focused and strategic. Jesus went where people lived.

He spent much of His time in towns, synagogues, and the town market. He attracted crowds but then took the time to minister to them. They were tired, hungry and thirsty. Jesus met their spiritual need and ministered to them physically as well. Jesus was present with them. Jesus did not hide Himself from the world but came and loved the people in it.

Many Christians are satisfied to be locked down in their holy huddles. They are content with isolating themselves from those who need God. It is safe, easy, and comfortable to be with other believers. There is a place and time for fellowship with other believers (more on that next week), but God has given us a command that we cannot disobey. The command is to GO! The church has done a great job when she gathers. Most churches know how to worship well. They may have a great music program, sound preaching, and lovely facilities. However, the power of the church, I believe, is seen the most, not when she is gathered but when she is scattered. When we put the light on the stand and make it visible, we will have the power to impact the world with God's light. What is the "stand" that you can place your lamp upon? Is it visible to those around you? Have you ever considered that you are a missionary? If you don't consider yourself a missionary, then why not?

DISCUSSION QUESTIONS

1. Why does Jesus emphasize the importance of making the light visible rather than hiding it? In what ways can we strategically place our light so that it has the most impact on darkness?

2. How does this teaching challenge traditional views of missionary work as simply sending money away? What can we learn from Jesus' approach to being near and engaging with those apart from God?

3. How did Jesus' mission of seeking and saving the lost shape His interactions with people? What specific actions did Jesus take to be present and minister to the needs of those around Him?

4. How can embracing your identity as a missionary change your perspective on everyday interactions? What steps can you take to live out your missional identity more fully?

5. How does making your light visible contribute to the power of the church when it is scattered? Share a time when you placed your light on a stand and made a visible impact on those around you.

DAY 17
THE LIGHT OF GOOD WORKS

In the same way, let your light shine before others, so that they may see your good works and give glory to your Father who is in heaven. - Matthew 5:16

Only some people who do good work do it with good intentions. This is because the praise of men easily sways our hearts. The Bible has commanded us to obey God and keep His commandments. However, this can only be possible when the gospel has transformed our hearts to obey. In this verse, Jesus explains that the purpose of doing "good works" is not for our benefit. The express purpose of every good work is for the world to see and glorify God. That sounds very elementary. Yet, so many Christians do not act as if they believe this to be true.

This may surprise you, but the purpose of sharing our faith is not for our church to grow numerically. Of course, it would be wonderful if the Lord chose for that to happen because we would want more people under the influence of the Word of God. No, the purpose of doing good works is so that people will glorify God. Sadly, much "evangelism" today is done as gimmicky church marketing. When a typical person says they "shared their faith," it usually means that they invited someone to their church. Inviting people to worship is a great thing! However, unless you are sharing Jesus, you aren't evangelizing. Evangelism is not bringing more people to your church but getting people to Jesus. I was caught in this mentality early in my ministry. I thought doing good community work would make our church look good to the lost. I was doing good work but with bad intentions. I did it for the church's glory and me as its pastor so that we would be well-known and people would attend.

God has not commanded us to do good works for the applause of others. He has commanded us to do good works so that others may see Him. This requires a radical shift in our hearts and minds. It's a humbling thought that God can use the "good" we do for Him to save those who believe. This doesn't mean we should stop doing good works, but we must constantly check our motives. Are we doing these good works for the glory of God, or for our own recognition?

A few years ago, I lent my neighbor my lawn tractor to help him cut his lawn. I had seen him struggle in the hot Florida sun and decided to offer my assistance. He eventually took me up on the offer and started using the tractor, making his job much more manageable. I had no hidden agenda; I saw a need and knew I could help. A few months later, this same neighbor was at my doorstep, distraught over personal relationship struggles. I was able to speak with him and share the gospel. He believed and was saved. This event forever changed how I saw good works being used for God's glory. The simple act of lending a lawn tractor allowed me to build a bridge. God softened his heart and called him to salvation. This is the potential impact of our good works when done with the right motives. How can you have a similar impact in your neighborhood? Can God use your good works as a light to show people the gospel? May the light of good works find proper motivation in your life to glory in God.

DISCUSSION QUESTIONS

1. According to the passage, what is the primary purpose of doing good works?

2. Share a time when you did a good work with pure intentions and saw a positive impact as a result.
How can simple acts of kindness, like lending a lawn tractor, be used by God to open doors for sharing the gospel?

3. Why do you think the praise of men can so easily sway our hearts when doing good works?

4. What is the difference between true evangelism and inviting people to church for numerical growth? How can we shift our focus from growing our church to genuinely sharing Jesus with others?

5. What are some specific ways you can build bridges in your neighborhood or community?

DAY 18
THE GOSPEL OF THE KINGDOM

And Jesus went throughout all the cities and villages, teaching in their synagogues and proclaiming the gospel of the kingdom and healing every disease and every affliction. - Matthew 9:35

We do not need to look to another example of being a missionary other than the person and work of Christ. Jesus' ministry did not begin when He went public at age thirty. It began before time began, as the Father purposed to redeem His people through His Son. God became a man. That is where the missionary story of Jesus begins. God took on flesh and blood and experienced what we experienced, yet without sin. God lived on earth amongst humanity and breathed the same air we breathe. Jesus grew up and had brothers and sisters, parents, and responsibilities. He had to learn, study, and experience puberty and young adulthood. He had friends, enemies, stalkers, and backstabbers. He knew how to be mistreated, mocked, lied about, accused falsely, and betrayed. When Jesus saw people, He knew what they were experiencing. He ministered to them from an understanding of who they were and what they had been through, just like we do in our daily lives. His experiences make Him relatable to us, and we can find comfort in the fact that He understands our struggles. Jesus was the greatest missionary who ever lived!

God's missionary work is not detached from names and faces. God's missionary work is not about numbers, lists, or prospects. Jesus knew people's names (Zacchaeus, Luke 19:1-10), their past (woman at the well, John 4), and their present needs. Matthew tells us that Jesus went "throughout all the cities and villages." Jesus went to where the people were. What did he do in these cities and villages? He taught and healed whomever He encountered. Jesus compassionately and lovingly met the needs of the people to whom He was sent.

Sadly, though, many believers are detached from the same kind of passionate connection with a dying and lost world. We have become contented as a culture to watch from afar and let the world turn as if Jesus never came. Jesus modeled for us a radical lifestyle of loving, serving, and showing truth to everyone. This lifestyle of sacrificial ministry was not comfortable. Jesus traveled around, often hungry, thirsty, and tired.

How can we engage with the needs of our city? How can we bring light to the darkness? If we're not fully engaging with our cities with a heartfelt need and compassion, we're missing out on what God is doing to build His Kingdom. We need to consider what it means for us to live in our cities as missionaries. Will we be solely focused on having the crowds come to us, or will we lovingly go to where the crowds are and give them the only hope that will transform their broken hearts? What changes do we need to make, both as a church and personally, to make this a reality? Let's change our rally cry from a "come to us" to a "we are going to you." Each one of us has a role to play in this mission, and it's time we take our responsibilities seriously. The time to act is now, and the urgency of this mission should inspire and motivate us to act immediately.

DISCUSSION QUESTIONS

1. How does Jesus' life and ministry serve as the ultimate example of being a missionary?

2. What does it mean that God's missionary work is not detached from names and faces? How did Jesus show personal connection and compassion in His ministry (e.g., Zacchaeus, the woman at the well)?

3. Why do you think many believers today are detached from a passionate connection with a dying and lost world? What are some challenges we face in engaging with our communities, and how can we overcome them?

4. What role do you personally play in this mission, and how can you take your responsibilities seriously? Reflect on your own life. What changes do you need to make to engage more effectively in missionary work?

5. How can we develop a heartfelt need and compassion for the people in our cities? What practical steps can we take to show compassion and meet the needs of those around us?

DAY 19
THE COMPASSION OF THE KINGDOM

When he saw the crowds, he had compassion for them, because they were harassed and helpless, like sheep without a shepherd. - Matthew 9:36

We need new eyes. We may have grown so accustomed to our surroundings that we miss the obvious. A few years ago, on the TV show Deal or No Deal, there was an episode that brought home the truth about this point. Deal or No Deal is a game show where contestants can make more money by selecting the correct briefcases. The models hold up the selected briefcases and show the contestants what they have won or didn't win. In one episode, there was a contestant whose family had arranged for her sister to appear as one of these models. The contestant did not realize her sister was on stage during the show. She kept playing the game and had no idea. Finally, after some time, the show's host decided to point out the model in hopes of the contestant realizing it was her sister. After being shown the model and asked explicitly if she noticed anything different about her, she was still clueless. Suddenly, it dawned on her that this was her sister! She hadn't seen her in about a year.

Many of us are like this contestant. We are not looking for ways to reach people; we miss the prominent God-given appointments. To see things differently, we need to ask God to awaken us. We need to see people in the way God does. God does not see people as prospects or potential people He could love. Jesus looked out over the crowds, following and listening to each word. He saw them as harassed and helpless. They needed Him, and He knew it. He could easily have dismissed them. He could have just let them wallow in the messes that they created by their sin. He could have wished somebody else to minister to them. He didn't. Matthew tells us that He was moved with compassion.

Compassion is a very interesting word. The literal definition of this word is "to be moved in the bowels." In the 1st century, the bowels were the seat of the emotions. In our modern culture, we use the word "heart." I love my wife with all of my "heart." Jesus, as He was looking at the crowds, was moved in His gut because He loved these people—biblical compassion results in action. Jesus did not feel sorry for them and then forgot about them the next day. Jesus was moved with compassion, and then He saved them. To feel sorry for somebody is not compassionate. It is a passive feeling of sympathy. Conversely, compassion is an active response to someone's suffering, motivated by love and a desire to alleviate their pain.

It's not enough to simply feel sorry for people. We must be moved to action, to do something that will make a real difference. Who is it that comes to your mind today? For whom have you felt pity but not genuine biblical compassion? Whether you are moved in your bowels or heart, it's time to act. Jesus did, and we serve in His strength. Let's not just feel compassion, let's live it through our actions. Let's bring His love and compassion to those in need. Let us know to miss the most obvious opportunities staring at us in the face.

DISCUSSION QUESTIONS

1. Have you ever missed something obvious in your surroundings, similar to the contestant on Deal or No Deal? Share your experience. How can we become more aware of the people and opportunities around us that we might be overlooking?

2. Why do you think we sometimes miss God-given opportunities to reach out to others? How can we stay alert and open to these opportunities in our daily lives?

3. What does it mean that Jesus was "moved in His bowels" with compassion? How does this differ from mere sympathy?

4. Who is someone in your life that you have felt pity for but have not yet acted with genuine compassion? What steps can you take to change that?

5. What is the danger of helping someone physically but not sharing Christ with them? Can acts of compassion be a hinderance to the gospel?

DAY 20
THE WORKERS OF THE KINGDOM

Then he said to his disciples, "The harvest is plentiful, but the laborers are few; therefore pray earnestly to the Lord of the harvest to send out laborers into his harvest." - Matthew 9:37-38

Some things never change. There always seems to be more work to do than people to do the work. This was no different in Jesus' day. He spoke to His disciples after Jesus saw the people and was moved with compassion. His plea to them was not a guilt trip. His plea seems extremely simple. He told the disciples to pray. Pray? That doesn't seem logical to attack the problem. We love to take the reins and take control of the situation. We want to be the hero who does what nobody else wants to do. I have often heard this passage preached, and it usually is from a guilt-laden perspective. Jesus doesn't burden people with guilt. He doesn't heap upon them something that is beyond them. He asks them to pray to the Lord of the Harvest.

When we pray to the Lord of the Harvest, we acknowledge that He is the one overseeing this mission. He is far greater, more powerful, and more capable than we could ever be. We are not worthy, capable, or strong enough to save anyone. But the Lord of the Harvest is different. This is His harvest, and He will ensure that His harvest comes in. Just as a farmer does not waste his crops, the Lord will not waste His harvest. We are not the Lord, but we are His valued and important laborers in His mission.

Instead of just talking about missions, let's talk to the God of the Mission. This is what Jesus commands us to do. He wants us to pray earnestly for the Lord to send out more laborers to gather the harvest. Prayer is not just a formality, it's the first step in our mission. It's our direct line to God, empowering us to be ready to act when called. This God-centered approach requires a faith far beyond our capabilities. It requires us to let God be God and understand that He alone is Sovereign to save. When the Lord of the Harvest calls us to go labor - we must go! Let's not just talk, let's pray and act.

There are millions of people without a gospel witness amongst them. Some people have no churches, Christians, or Bibles. How will they hear without a preacher? How will they hear without one being sent? How will our city be impacted by the gospel if we are not continually falling on our faces and asking the Lord to call people to repentance? As the gospel reigns in our hearts, we can be a light to share Christ!! May the gospel advance through the light of the prayers of God's people. Pray to the Lord of the harvest!

DISCUSSION QUESTIONS

1. Why do you think Jesus instructed His disciples to pray rather than immediately act when He saw the people in need? How does this instruction challenge our natural inclination to take control and be the "hero"?

2. How does recognizing God's sovereignty in the mission help us understand our role as laborers?

3. How can we balance understanding that God is the one who oversees the mission while also recognizing our important role as laborers?

4. What does the metaphor of the harvest teach us about the urgency and importance of mission work? How can we better understand and appreciate the concept of the harvest in our prayer and mission efforts?

5. Share a story or testimony of how prayer has led to impactful mission work or the sending of laborers. How can these stories encourage and motivate us to continue praying earnestly?

DAY 21
SONS OF YOUR FATHER

"You have heard that it was said, 'You shall love your neighbor and hate your enemy.' But I say to you, Love your enemies and pray for those who persecute you, so that you may be sons of your Father who is in heaven. For he makes his sun rise on the evil and on the good, and sends rain on the just and on the unjust. For if you love those who love you, what reward do you have? Do not even the tax collectors do the same? And if you greet only your brothers, what more are you doing than others? Do not even the Gentiles do the same? You therefore must be perfect, as your heavenly Father is perfect." Matthew 9:43-48

My children love Apple products. I am not speaking about pies, juice, or sauces. I am talking about Apple, Inc., the Cupertino, California company that puts out Macintosh computers, iPhones, iPods, iPads and more. My children have this love and appreciation of Apple because they know that I love Apple. I talk about Apple, use their products, and have shown them the benefits of being an Apple consumer. I downplayed the competition (Microsoft, Google) and argued why Apple was superior. They are growing up in my home and imitate, love, and appreciate the things that their Dad loves. It doesn't stop with Apple; they have also picked up on my mannerisms, sayings, and love for other things. This runs in the family. They look like me, talk like me, and enjoy the things I love. People know they are my children because they love and live the same things I love. This is one piece of evidence that they are my children.

This is not much different than our relationship with God. If we are indeed His, we will imitate, and act like Him. When God saved us, He began conforming us to the image of Jesus. He created me in His image (Genesis 1:26) and shaped me to be just like Jesus (Romans 8:29). Our light shines best when we yield to His Spirit and obey His commandments. This is not possible within our strength. Many try to fool others by acting morally. You can change your exterior without much work. You can fool almost everyone by pretending to be good. However, true righteousness comes from an overflow of God working within you!

This is what Jesus is addressing in Matthew 9. He is teaching the disciples that the world expects us to hate our enemies and love our neighbors. But the working of God within my heart frees me to love my enemies as well! This is radical. The purpose of loving our enemies is to show that we are "sons of our Father." How will our city know that we are His? We won't have to prove we are from the Father; it will be impossible to hide it. How are you living your life? Does your life proclaim that the tomb is empty or occupied? Does your life give evidence of Jesus being alive, or is He still dead? My children love and act the way I do because they are in my family! What does your heart or actions say about who you belong to? Because we belong to Him, the Light of the City shines down upon this world!

DISCUSSION QUESTIONS

1. How does our relationship with God parallel the way children imitate their parents?

2. What does it mean to be conformed to the image of Jesus according to Romans 8:29?

3. What is the difference between outward moral behavior and true righteousness that comes from God working within us? Why is it important to have an internal transformation rather than just external behavior changes?

WEEK 4

THE LIGHT
OF LOVE

DAY 22
LOVE ONE ANOTHER

"A new commandment I give to you, that you love one another: just as I have loved you, you also are to love one another. By this all people will know that you are my disciples, if you have love for one another." (John 13:34-35)

The one thing missing from most churches is genuine, sacrificial love for God's people. Jesus said that one of the fruits that will prove who we are is our love for each other. Jesus spoke this directly to His disciples. The light of love shines from the church when the church acts like the church. Because of the internet, we are a more connected society than ever before. People spend countless hours throughout the year on Facebook and Twitter "connecting" and "sharing" with one another. I would venture to say that we have never been more connected but have never been lonelier. Social media websites are practical and helpful. However, social media interaction is just scratching the surface of human connection. It is great to have people comment on your latest status update on Facebook. Having somebody "retweet" something you said on Twitter is even rewarding. However, we were made for much deeper social connectivity.

The word "community" might be a little foreign to some. I am not speaking about the community "neighborhood" in which we live. I am speaking to those to whom we relate on a deeper level. Attending church on Sunday is needed as we worship with the larger church family and hear the preached Word. However, we need the dependence, trust, and engagement of others. If we only see each other on Sunday, it will be hard to truly "love one another."

You need to find those in whom you can sacrificially practice this kind of love. What love? Interestingly, Jesus has set the standard high. How are we to love one another? He says, "Just as I have loved you." You can't outlove Jesus. We have set the bar too low in our pursuit of loving God's people. Most interaction among Christians is very superficial and shallow. For instance, discussing the weather or the latest sports game. That is fun, entertaining, and helpful. But if our connection does not go any further, we will be in trouble.

Let us love each other as Jesus loves us! Let us look for ways and opportunities to exercise our spiritual "muscles." The commands that we have toward one another do not end with love. The New Testament is filled with ways we are commanded to exhibit true Biblical community, which involves sacrificial love, mutual support, and accountability. We will focus on some of these commands for the rest of this week. Let the light of His love ignite us to love each other so the world will see and glorify Him! Who do you need to be more loving to in your church family?

DISCUSSION QUESTIONS

1. What does Jesus mean by loving one another "just as I have loved you"? How can we practice genuine, sacrificial love within our church communities?

2. How do you define "community" in the context of the church? How is it different from simply attending church services? Why is building deeper connections within the church community beyond Sunday services essential?

3. Can you think of examples from your own life or others where sacrificial love was demonstrated within the church community? How did these acts of love impact the individuals involved and the broader community?

4. What are some specific New Testament commands regarding how we should treat one another in the church? How can we actively implement these commands in our daily lives and church activities?

5. What steps can you take to be more engaged and connected with your church family?

DAY 23
ACCEPT ONE ANOTHER

May the God who gives endurance and encouragement give you the same attitude of mind toward each other that Christ Jesus had, so that with one mind and one voice you may glorify the God and Father of our Lord Jesus Christ. Accept one another, then, just as Christ accepted you, in order to bring praise to God. - Romans 15:7 (NIV)

This week, we will look closely at some of the "spiritual exercises" commanded for the church. Yesterday, we saw how we are commanded to love one another. Love is the foundation for all the exercises that we will discuss. Love is the foundation and fuel for all that a believer does. God loves us, and His love overflows our hearts to impact the world around us. Near the end of his letter to the Romans, Paul admonishes these early Christians to "accept one another." Acceptance of Christians almost seems too elementary to include in this 40-day journey.

Just as our benchmark for love is Christ, so is our standard for acceptance. We are instructed to love one another as Christ loved us! Similarly, we are called to accept one another as Christ has accepted us. This means welcoming new members, forgiving past mistakes, and supporting each other in need. Paul informed these early Christians that this practice brings much praise and glory to God.

Let's celebrate it. People are unique. No two individuals are alike, and we should be grateful for that. We must recognize and rejoice in the diversity that God has bestowed upon us in Christ. It's a joyous part of our faith journey. God has given each of us in Christ. Because of His mercy, He overlooked our flaws and chose us unconditionally in Christ before the world began. God did not choose us based on our works, looks, or talents. There was nothing lovely, exciting, or profitable about us. He accepted us because He is holy, loving, and kind. His acceptance is unwavering and unconditional, bringing us comfort and reassurance.

A church comprises a group of born-again believers accepted by the Father in Christ. These people can be from all different walks of life. Some people may have been saved as a child, while others have walked a dark past. This is crucial for the acceptance that God has given us in Him. No matter the walk of life, we all need the same grace and acceptance. A healthy church will have a great mix of elderly and young believers. All this magnificent work is found in the person of Christ. When we come together and see the diverse group He has joined, it brings much praise to Him. The urgency and significance of accepting one another cannot be overstated. Are we accepting of one another? Do we see past age, skin color, background, and economic status? If you struggle with accepting one another, I urge you to celebrate the grace that God has given you. You are no better or more deserving than anyone else. Who do you need to be more accepting of within your church family?

DISCUSSION QUESTIONS

1. What does it mean to accept one another as Christ has accepted us?

2. Are there people within your church community that you find difficult to accept? Why? How can you work on overcoming these difficulties and embracing others as Christ does?

3. How can we move beyond superficial interactions to build genuine, deep relationships within the church?

DAY 24
SERVE ONE ANOTHER

For you were called to freedom, brothers. Only do not use your freedom as an opportunity for the flesh, but through love serve one another. For the whole law is fulfilled in one word: "You shall love your neighbor as yourself." But if you bite and devour one another, watch out that you are not consumed by one another. Gal 5:13-15

We are a selfish people. This is the way my heart is designed to operate from birth. I want people to applaud, notice, and serve me. I want my needs to be met and others to pay attention to me. This way of living will swallow you alive and leave you depressed. But there is a better way to live. This way contradicts my natural desires. This way is only accomplished through the gospel's transformative power, which can shine light on my dark heart and change me from within. This is why the gospel must be a work of God within my heart. Sure, I can pretend to serve other people first. It is very much impossible to selflessly want to serve and love other people in my own strength. I can fake it for a little bit, but eventually, it will sneak up on me, and I'll be found out. I can't depend on myself to love, serve, or give to others out of pure motivation. I must trust in God's radical transformation to change me into the person that He wants me to become.

How can you serve one another in your church family? How can we be a blessing? It is easier to meet other people's needs if you are watching out for how to do so. How attentive are you to the hurts and needs of others? You can only serve if you know who to serve. All it takes is listening ears or watchful eyes. The Bible says that Jesus watched the crowds multiple times in the gospels. Jesus spent time listening and watching. He spent time with His disciples and knew them thoroughly. This is why you must belong to a church! We must be around other Christians to accomplish these "one another" commands we see throughout the New Testament. Yes, you can worship independently, but you can't live that way. Belonging to a church community is not just about attending services; it's about sharing life and serving one another. It's about finding a place where you belong, are loved and accepted, and can love and serve others in return.

The early church knew this kind of life. We are told in the book of Acts that they met daily for fellowship and worship. They spent significant amounts of time together. We are told that there was no need amongst them. Why? They sold their possessions and gave them to everyone who needed it. That is a sacrificial, always-thinking-about-others kind of love. That is the kind of love the gospel produces in us to serve one another. How open are your eyes? How

tuned are your ears? Does someone hurt among us?
Pray for the Lord to give you awareness. Serve one
another!

DISCUSSION QUESTIONS

1. How can you cultivate a habit of being more attentive to those around you?

2. How does the early church in the book of Acts serve as a model for community living and sacrificial love? What steps can we take to foster a similar sense of community and support in our own church?

3. What are some common barriers that prevent us from serving others selflessly? How can we overcome these barriers and develop a heart of genuine service?

DAY 25
BEAR ONE ANOTHER

Brothers, if anyone is caught in any transgression, you who are spiritual should restore him in a spirit of gentleness. Keep watch on yourself, lest you too be tempted. Bear one another's burdens, and so fulfill the law of Christ. For if anyone thinks he is something, when he is nothing, he deceives himself. (Galatians 6:1-3)

This week, we have seen that we are responsible for each other. God has not called any one of us to do life alone. Some of us may never get married, have children, or live near relatives. But remember, you belong to God's family. In the church, you find love, relationships, and acceptance. I am compelled and empowered to think differently about other believers through the gospel. The Bible even teaches that we are in a special relationship with believers. We are the body of Christ. This body is a living, breathing organism that has its existence through, for, and because of God's glory. So, with this in mind, we live differently. We understand that we are not individually the church, but we are the church together.

Paul admonishes the Galatians to keep a watch for those who are falling into sin. Paul uses the word "caught." This word conveys someone who needs our help to be freed. This person Paul describes as stuck in habitual sin. Paul urges those who are mature to help those who are not in overcoming their addictions & problems. The command is to bear the burdens of those within our local church. To be a part of a church is to lean on others to help you become more Christ-like. This accountability is what we all need. It's a sign of our connectedness and care for one another.

Of course, this could be used badly in the church's life. Let me be very clear. God does not want us to be spiritual policemen. We do not need to live in fear of our brothers and sisters. We need to exercise biblical accountability with enormous and radical grace. When someone in our church comes with a burden of sin, we need to be prepared to show them the power of the gospel. It is the gospel that helps us bear the burden and the gospel that releases it. The light that shines from our gathering is the evidence of the gospel bearing fruit in our lives.

How is this culture created in our church? It comes with trust and authentic relationships. This is why small groups are so important. They provide a platform for us to foster these authentic relationships. Living out what God wants us to do is hard if we only meet on Sundays. We need each other to live this kind of "one another" life! We need to see each other often and outside the church walls. Whose burdens are you bearing? Whose life are you impacting with grace? This is what it means to be a part of a church family.

DISCUSSION QUESTIONS

1. What does it mean to be part of the body of Christ?

2. How does understanding that we are the church together, not individually, influence the way we live and interact with each other?

3. How can we help those who are "caught" in habitual sin, according to Paul's teachings to the Galatians?

DAY 26
BUILD ONE ANOTHER

For God has not destined us for wrath, but to obtain salvation through our Lord Jesus Christ, who died for us so that whether we are awake or asleep we might live with him. Therefore encourage one another and build one another up, just as you are doing. 1 Thessalonians 5:9-11

My prayer for you this week is that you will understand the implications of a gospel-centered church and life. Everything that we have read, written, and said these 40 days will be for nothing if we don't comprehend the power of the gospel. I am not speaking about becoming a Christian. I am talking about Christians understanding who they are because in Christ. All the commands of God have their completion for obedience in the power of the gospel. This is why Paul could say, "I have been crucified with Christ. It is no longer I who live, but Christ who lives in me. And the life I now live in the flesh I live by faith in the Son of God, who loved me and gave Himself for me." (Galatians 2:20)

This gospel is not my ticket into a club. It is a daily reminder of who we were and what we are becoming in Christ. It is a reminder that I have been saved from our sins, hell, and God's wrath. It reminds me that I now stand entirely accepted and approved before a Holy God. This gospel is not a stepping stone to the next level in Christianity. It encompasses all of Christianity. This gospel is so big that every story, on every page, whispers His name. This gospel needs to serve as our daily encouragement. To make this a reality, you need to preach the gospel to yourself daily.

In this passage, Paul tells the Thessalonians to encourage and build up one another. As believers, we have the responsibility to immerse others and ourselves in this refreshing gospel. We take our triumph through this message of hope and the soon-returning King. We are to encourage and build. We can do this through words, deeds, and our presence. The truth is that God has called all of us to this kind of gospel life. This is not just something that pastors are told to do. This is something for the body of Christ to do and to accomplish together. Many Christians and churches do just the opposite.

God desires to use us to build other people up! We are all called to invest. This is what makes a church a church. It is God's people journeying and covenanting together to make a difference in each other and the world. Who have you been building up? Let us not shy away from being repetitious with the gospel of God's glorious grace! Invest the power of the gospel into your heart and the lives of others today!

DISCUSSION QUESTIONS

1. How does Galatians 2:20 reflect our new identity in Christ?

2. Why is it important to preach the gospel to yourself daily? How can we make the gospel a daily encouragement in our lives?

3. According to Paul, why is it essential for believers to encourage and build up one another?

4. What does it mean to be repetitious with the gospel of God's glorious grace?

5. Who in your life have you been actively building up with the gospel? How have you done this? What are some challenges you face in building up others, and how can you overcome them?

DAY 27
TEACH ONE ANOTHER

Let the word of Christ dwell in you richly, teaching and admonishing one another in all wisdom, singing psalms and hymns and spiritual songs, with thankfulness in your hearts to God. - Colossians 3:16

Being a part of a gospel-centered church motivates us to teach each other. We must be passionate about this responsibility. Most churches have the mindset that the church only has one teacher. It is not just the pastor's job to disciple people. Jesus has called all of us to be disciples and disciplers! This biblical mandate will not change until He returns. Every single one of us needs someone to disciple us, and at the same time we need to have someone we are discipling. We need always to be teaching and learning.

How does this happen? I don't know about you, but I go through periods of dryness. I feel like the wind has been knocked out of me, and I have nothing to give. Sometimes, it may feel like we are just going through the motions and stuck in a giant rut. I think there are often many reasons for experiencing seasons of life like this. We may have an unconfessed sin or go through a "gospel amnesia." Gospel amnesia is a state where we forget the gospel's transformative power in our lives and start believing the lies we tell ourselves. The answer lies within Paul's Holy Spirit-inspired words to the Colossians. Paul urges them to "Let the word of Christ dwell in you richly." Within that opening statement comes the power we need to teach others. I know what some of you are thinking. "Dan, I am not a teacher. I could never get in front of a group of people and teach them! After all, I've never been to Bible College or seminary!"

You are wrong. God never commanded anybody to go to seminary or Bible College. This command is given to believers who have never had any higher education. Yet, Paul commands them to do what most of you think you cannot do. We don't realize that we teach more with our lives than with our mouths. What you do has much more weight than what you say. The power to teach others does not come from how well you understand the message. It has nothing to do with how many Bible verses or facts you may have memorized. The power to teach and to admonish comes from letting the "word of Christ dwell richly" within you.

The light of the word dwelling richly has the power to teach others. The word that lives within me produces the richness of my soul. You can teach others as you have been taught. After all, your pastor is not your ultimate teacher. The Holy Spirit that indwells you is your Teacher. I don't teach you anything. The Holy Spirit uses the words that come from my mouth, takes those words, and connects the dots within our hearts and minds. This work of the Spirit within me has the power to teach other people. May our church be filled with this Spirit so that others are taught, encouraged, and admonished. This is not a passive command. It is intentional. Who are you learning from? Who are you teaching? Is the word dwelling richly within your heart? within your heart?

DISCUSSION QUESTIONS

1. Why is it essential for everyone in the church, not just the pastor, to be involved in discipleship?

2. What does it mean to be both a disciple and a discipler? How can we create a culture in our church where everyone is actively involved in teaching and learning?

3. What does it mean to "let the word of Christ dwell in you richly"? How does this command from Paul empower us to teach and disciple others effectively?

DAY 28
CONFESS TO ONE ANOTHER

Is anyone among you suffering? Let him pray. Is anyone cheerful? Let him sing praise. Is anyone among you sick? Let him call for the elders of the church, and let them pray over him, anointing him with oil in the name of the Lord. And the prayer of faith will save the one who is sick, and the Lord will raise him up. And if he has committed sins, he will be forgiven. Therefore, confess your sins to one another and pray for one another, that you may be healed. The prayer of a righteous person has great power as it is working. Elijah was a man with a nature like ours, and he prayed fervently that it might not rain, and for three years and six months it did not rain on the earth. Then he prayed again, and heaven gave rain, and the earth bore its fruit. - James 5:13-18

This week, we have read about the responsibilities the Bible urges us to exercise toward one another. In review, we have covered that we are responsible for loving, accepting, serving, building, carrying, and teaching. These commands are just scratching the surface of the privileges of being a part of a biblical community. They are not a burden to weigh us down, but a joy to obey. When we live this kind of grace life, the light of love best impacts darkness.

The least used power in the world is prayer. It's a powerful resource that we often neglect. Biblical relationships demand that we pray for one another. Praying for one another is an act of love. It demonstrates that we truly desire what is best for each other. Let's not underestimate the power of prayer, and let's use it to show our love for one another. Why don't we pray more?

1. We don't pray because we are too "busy." We have become extremely busy people who have drowned ourselves in busy lives. If you are too busy to pray, you are too busy! Busyness never stopped Martin Luther from praying. Martin Luther once said, "I have so much to do today that I'm going to need to spend three hours in prayer to get it all done."[1]

2. We don't pray for others because we never meant it. Another reason we struggle to pray for others because we never really meant to pray. It might be that "I'll pray for you" has just become a cliché." I'll pray for you" is the proper response to someone asking for prayer. But do we mean it? Or has it become something we say when we don't know what else to say? Is it possible that you just said that because you felt you were supposed to? Did we only say it to make ourselves

[1] 1. http://www.christianitytoday.com/moi/2011/006/december/too- busy-not-to-pray.html

sound more spiritual? Or maybe we were saying it to make them feel better? Praying for others, also known as intercessory prayer, is a powerful act of love. It involves lifting the needs and concerns of others to God, asking for His intervention and blessing in their lives.

How do we change this? How can we pray for each other more often? It sounds simple, but the easiest way is to write it down. I am much more likely to remember to pray for that person if I write it down. In addition to writing it down, why not just pray on the spot for the person? This way, you can keep your promise to pray if you pause to pray on the spot with the person. The light of love can be seen as we pray for one another!

DISCUSSION QUESTIONS

1. Why do you think prayer is often the least used power in the world?

2. In what ways does praying for one another demonstrate true love? Can you share a time when someone's prayers made a significant impact on your life?

3. Do you identify with the reasons given for why people don't pray more (being too busy, not meaning it)? Why or why not?

WEEK 5

THE LIGHT OF THE GOSPEL

DAY 29
THE GOSPEL REVEALS JESUS

"But when he who had set me apart before I was born, and who called me by his grace, was pleased to reveal his Son to me, in order that I might preach him among the Gentiles..." - Gal 1:15-16

When I was a youth pastor, my "cool factor" went up a "hundredfold" when I used a black light during teen group. It did not add any spiritual blessings, but they connected with it. Teenagers are somehow more engaged by things that look out of the ordinary. The black light revealed things that could not be seen with normal light, making even certain things glow. Black lights emanate an ultraviolet light, which is not visible but reveals things in the darkness. The gospel is very much like this ultra-violet light. The gospel will reveal much that can only be seen by its light. This week, we will explore the various gospel revelations shown.

First and foremost, the gospel reveals Jesus. The gospel begins with Jesus, and it continues in and through Him. The gospel is personal. Many people love to devote much attention to the "facts" of the gospel.

The gospel is much more than facts. Neither is it a method or a mission. The gospel is a person. On the Damascus road, Paul encountered the person of Jesus. He fell and was blinded so that he could not see. Why? He had encountered Jesus in His Glory. He did not encounter a belief system, a church, or a religion. He discovered God in human likeness.

In the letter to the Galatians, Paul spends much time defending the gospel because of false teachers. He also shares his testimony about what the gospel revealed to him. God the Father revealed "His Son" to Paul. This was done before Paul was born, and it happened because of God calling Paul by His grace. Paul met Jesus that day on the Damascus Road, resulting from a merciful God who would use Paul for His glory. If the gospel you believe leads you anywhere else but the person of Christ, you don't believe the gospel of the Bible.

There is much talk of the supposed "prosperity gospel" on TV by greedy televangelists. The gospel that they preach is no gospel at all. The gospel they preach has God reveal to us money, health, and wealth. It is no wonder that many of these men and women live outrageous lifestyles with the contributions of their supporters. Their love of money has become their god. Their success has been elevated beyond their proper reality to idolatrous proportions. Their gospel is not the biblical gospel of grace, which leads them to Christ, but to themselves. In much contrast, John Piper wisely wrote, "God is the gospel."[2] He is right. We are saved so that we can have a relationship with God. The blessing of being saved is not that I escape Hell but that I get God. God is the blessing of salvation. Salvation is about a person, not a place. The gospel light always reveals and points to Jesus.

[2] 1. John Piper, God is the Gospel: Meditations on God's Love as the Gift of Himself. (Wheaton, Illinois: Nashville: Published by Crossway Books A publishing ministry of Good News Publishers. 1300 Crescent Street, Wheaton, Illinois 60187 Piper, John (2008-04-07). Kindle Edition.

DISCUSSION QUESTIONS

1. Why is it important to understand that the gospel begins with and is centered around Jesus? How does viewing the gospel as a person rather than just facts or a method change our approach to faith?

2. How does Paul's testimony about God revealing His Son to him before he was born demonstrate the power of God's grace?

3. John Piper stated, "God is the gospel." What does this mean, and why is it significant?

4. What are some common misconceptions about the gospel that we need to address when sharing our faith?

DAY 30
THE GOSPEL REVEALS
RIGHTEOUSNESS

For I am not ashamed of the gospel, for it is the power of God for salvation to everyone who believes, to the Jew first and also to the Greek. For in it the righteousness of God is revealed from faith for faith, as it is written, "The righteous shall live by faith." Romans 1:16-17

Paul loved the gospel. Paul always wrote with the focal point on the power of God to save sinners. The gospel is "the power of God." This gospel is so powerful that it transforms dead and wicked hearts. This happens because, as Paul says, "the righteousness of God is revealed." Through the gospel, we can begin to see His beauty and majesty. The fact that God is righteous reveals to us our desperate wickedness. Yes, you are wicked. You may not be as bad (humanly speaking) as Adolf Hitler, Osama Bin Laden, or a serial killer, but the Bible says that we all have a wicked heart. If you disagree, it's because your heart is deceiving you. "The heart is deceitful above all things, and desperately wicked: who can know it?" (Jeremiah 17:9 KJV)

Only God can fathom the depths of our depravity. Only God can truly comprehend the state of our hearts. When the light of God's gospel penetrates our hearts, it exposes our ugliness and His ultimate worth. If you find the magnitude of your wickedness hard to accept, it's because you have not fully grasped the magnitude of His righteousness. Yes, this gospel can be offensive and foolish to some, but it is God's tool to save those who believe.

There is a temptation to add our power to the gospel as if God needed our 'power' or knowledge to save sinners. When we focus on our power to save others, we dilute the gospel. You and I are not even powerful or worthy enough to save ourselves. What makes us think that we could save someone else? The gospel story is marvelously profound yet beautifully simple. God is righteous and worthy of all worship. We, on the other hand, are not worthy, but we often think we are, and in doing so, we steal His glory by living the way we want. Until you recognize how much more worthy God is than you, you cannot fully comprehend the depths of the gospel. Like a black light in a dark room, the gospel reveals things that were always there but not visible. It shows us that we cannot see for ourselves. We are conditioned to believe that we are ultimately worthy and honorable. We think we don't need God because we have it all figured out without him. Does this sound like you or someone you know? God transforms our hearts with His gospel by making us see He is all we need. He is the answer. This is all of grace.

If you struggle to see your need for God today, know you are not alone. Many of us have been where you are. I ask you to pray. Ask Him right now to help you understand. I pray that the barriers keeping you from believing will be removed. May your heart be open to the beauty of the gospel that shines the light of His glory on your need for Him. The gospel reveals a Righteous God who is worthy, Holy, and mighty to save.

DISCUSSION QUESTIONS

1. What does it mean that the gospel is "the power of God"? How have you seen the transformative power of the gospel in your life or the lives of others?

2. How does the gospel reveal both God's righteousness and our wickedness? Why is it important to understand our own depravity in order to fully grasp the magnitude of God's righteousness?

3. Reflect on Jeremiah 17:9. How does understanding the deceitfulness of the heart impact your view of yourself and others? In what ways can we guard against being deceived by our own hearts?

DAY 31
THE GOSPEL REVEALS GOD'S WRATH

"For the wrath of God is revealed from heaven against all ungodliness and unrighteousness of men, who by their unrighteousness suppress the truth." - Romans 1:18

Some will attempt to share the "gospel" while focusing on all the so-called "good" parts. This is a foolish attempt and is not faithful to the gospel revealed in the scriptures. Almost everyone talks about God's love for the world in His salvation of sinners. This is true. God did, in fact, "so loved the world" (John 3:16), but that is not the whole story. Paul tells us here that the gospel that he is not "ashamed" to share also reveals something hard to swallow. The gospel reveals God's wrath. Paul tells us that the gospel speaks loudly about the "wrath of God revealed from heaven against all ungodliness of men." Sin always has a price.

If the gospel were just about God's love, Jesus would not have had to sacrifice His life for us. John 3:16 says God "gave His one and only Son." This was not a new concept for the Jewish people. The forgiveness of sins always required a sacrifice. God commanded Israel to make a sacrifice to atone for sins. The sacrificial lamb did not escape the penalty of sin.

The lamb bore the penalty, as the priest obeyed God and offered the lamb on behalf of the people. The lamb had its throat slit and blood collected. This was to be an unmistakable symbol of the seriousness of sin against a Holy God. God, who is entirely righteous, has no sin.

Jesus did not just pay the price for sin; He WAS the price. Paul tells us in 2 Corinthians 5:21, "For our sake he made him to be sin who knew no sin so that in him we might become the righteousness of God." An innocent Jesus, who never sinned, became sin on the cross. He was the lamb who bore the punishment for the sins of a nation. He was the innocent, spotless, and perfect Lamb of God. The Father poured His wrath on the Son for our sins on that cross. This wrath-absorbing death was worse than the physical and emotional torture he endured. Did this take God by surprise? Nope. Paul tells us that God the Father planned it."...this Jesus, delivered up according to the definite plan and foreknowledge of God..." Acts 2:23

Isaiah prophesied that God the Father would be satisfied by it. "Yet it was the will of the Lord to crush him; he has put him to grief; when his soul makes an offering for guilt, he shall see his offspring; he shall prolong his days; the will of the Lord shall prosper in his hand. Out of the anguish of his soul, he shall see and be satisfied; by his knowledge, the righteous one, my servant, shall make many to be accounted righteous, and he shall bear their iniquities." (Isaiah 53:10-11)

Jesus cried out in agony as the wrath of His Father was being poured out on His body. Jesus endured the wrath of God. Jesus did not deserve the wrath of God. We are very deserving of it. We are the ones who should bear the price for our rebellion. Thankfully, the good news of the gospel is also in the wrath of God. We must keep sight of the gravity of this message. The gospel reveals that Jesus absorbed the full force of God's wrath due to me. The light of the gospel shows me that without the good news of the gospel, I would be receiving God's just wrath for my sins. This is humbling and makes grace all the sweeter.

DISCUSSION QUESTIONS

1. How does understanding the full scope of the gospel, including God's wrath, deepen our appreciation of God's love?

2. How do John 3:16 and Romans 1:18 complement each other in presenting a complete picture of the gospel? How can focusing only on God's love without acknowledging His wrath lead to a diluted understanding of the gospel?

3. How did Jesus' death on the cross satisfy God's wrath? Why is it significant that God's wrath was poured out on Jesus, and not us?

4. How does the reality of God's wrath and Jesus' sacrificial death humble us? In what ways does this understanding make God's grace all the more sweet and precious?

5. Reflect on 2 Corinthians 5:21. What does it mean that Jesus "became sin" for us? How does understanding that Jesus was the sacrificial lamb impact your view of sin and atonement?

☐

DAY 32
THE GOSPEL REVEALS REAL VICTORY

Read - 1 Corinthians 15

The message of the gospel does not have its completion at the cross. Some think they share the gospel by saying Jesus died on the cross. That is true; however, it is not the whole story. Jesus isn't dead. He is alive! Victory has its full expression in Jesus, who conquered sin, hell, and the grave. I can celebrate because in Jerusalem, the bones of Jesus cannot be found! People have tried to find Him, but "He isn't here. He has risen as He said." This is not just a "once a year" event to celebrate. Jesus' resurrection gives us hope every day. For the believer, every day is Resurrection Day!

"But God, being rich in mercy, because of the great love with which He loved us, even when we were dead in our trespasses, made us alive together with Christ — by grace you have been saved" Ephesians 2:4-5 Because of Christ, we also are raised from the dead at our salvation. Paul tells us that we were dead but have been raised to new life. The resurrection is vastly important because it shows what happens to every believer when they believe. We have been "made alive." We have

experienced the power of God in our lives because of Jesus' victory.

When I struggle with sin, I only need to remind myself of what Jesus has done. Jesus' victory over death conquers all my sins. It conquers the power of physical death. One day, I will physically die. But because Christ lives, I can confidently know that I will live again with Him! I can also have victory over spiritual death. Because I have been "made alive," I can know confidently that the gospel gives me victory over sin. Through the gospel, God changes my heart's affections to love Him more than I loved my sin. I was dead, but now I live!

If Jesus were still dead, we would have much to dread. Paul even went as far as to say that:

"And if Christ has not been raised, then our preaching is in vain and your faith is in vain. We are even found to be misrepresenting God, because we testified about God that he raised Christ, whom he did not raise if it is true that the dead are not raised. For if the dead are not raised, not even Christ has been raised. And if Christ has not been raised, your faith is futile, and you are still in your sins. Then, those who have fallen asleep in Christ also perished. If in Christ we have hope in this life only, we are of all people most to be pitied." (1 Corinthians 15:14-19)

We need to immerse ourselves in this gospel every day. As previously noted, "We need to preach the gospel to ourselves daily." What is the gospel? The gospel is the good news that Jesus died, was buried, and rose again from the dead. This is something that Paul declares as of "first importance" (1 Corinthians 15:1-4). Where do you place the gospel in your life? Was it something you did to get into the club, or is it the hope and power of your life? Remind yourself that the gospel reveals real victory. That victory has its exclamation in an empty tomb.

DISCUSSION QUESTIONS

1. Why is it important to understand that the message of the gospel does not end at the cross? How does the resurrection of Jesus complete the message of the gospel

2. How does Jesus' victory over sin, hell, and the grave impact your daily life and struggles with sin?

3. According to Ephesians 2:4-5, what does it mean to be made alive together with Christ? How does this new life in Christ transform our affections and desires?

4. What does Paul mean when he says that if Christ has not been raised, our faith is in vain (1 Corinthians 15:14-19)?

5. Why do we need to preach the gospel to ourselves daily? How can you make a habit of reminding yourself of the gospel's truth and power each day?

DAY 33
THE GOSPEL REVEALS REAL JOY

For I consider that the sufferings of this present time are not worth comparing with the glory that is to be revealed to us. For the creation waits with eager longing for the revealing of the sons of God. For the creation was subjected to futility, not willingly, but because of him who subjected it, in hope that the creation itself will be set free from its bondage to corruption and obtain the freedom of the glory of the children of God. For we know that the whole creation has been groaning together in the pains of childbirth until now. And not only the creation, but we ourselves, who have the firstfruits of the Spirit, groan inwardly as we wait eagerly for adoption as sons, the redemption of our bodies. For in this hope we were saved. Romans 8:18-24

Our souls crave happiness. Deep down, we know there is something better and greater to live for. We fill this void with many temporal and superficial things. It is the pursuit of happiness that drives us mad. Happiness is different for each of us. What makes me happy may not be what brings you happiness. Happiness changes from day to day and moment by moment. Everything can change for you in an instant. Happiness is dependent upon you and the people around you. Happiness always relies on people, places, or things to make and keep me happy. So, in vain, we try to sustain happiness in the long term, which is a fruitless effort. This is not the way God wants us to live.

God does not want you to be happy. God wants you to be joyful. What's the difference? Joy is what my soul craves. Joy cannot be manufactured or sustained by human effort. Joy is God produced. Joy is created and maintained by God in my heart. Joy is only found in God. The Joy of the Lord will get you through the darkest nights. The Joy of God will help you endure the days when things are collapsing all around you. This is why the Bible declares, "The joy of the Lord is my strength." People and circumstances may change, but God can be trusted in all the turmoil. It is in the gospel that true joy is revealed. The gospel reveals that my heart is empty without God. My idolatrous heart loves to replace Him and His joy with my temporary happiness. I then worship the happiness that brings me temporary relief from my pain. The absence of joy leaves the scars behind and leaves me craving and longing for more that I cannot satisfy. My heart will have sustainable and immeasurable joy only by being confident in God.

How could Paul sing in jail at midnight after being whipped? Or how could King David be on the run as a fugitive but still maintain a level of sanity? The joy of the Lord strengthens, enables, and empowers.

Paul tells us in this passage that the glories of the gospel are far better than what is happening to you and me. Creation is groaning, and so is my soul. It takes the light of the gospel to reveal to me this God-Centered joy. ☐

DISCUSSION QUESTIONS

1. Why do you think our souls crave happiness, and what drives this pursuit?

2. How do we often try to fill the void in our lives with temporal and superficial things?

3. What are the key differences between happiness and joy? Why is happiness often dependent on external factors, while joy is not?

4. Reflect on the statement, "The joy of the Lord is my strength." How has this truth been evident in your life?

5. How could Paul sing in jail at midnight after being whipped, and how does this illustrate the joy of the Lord?

DAY 34
THE GOSPEL REVEALS THE BIBLE

READ - Luke 24:13-27

"And he said to them, " O foolish ones, and slow of heart to believe all that the prophets have spoken! Was it not necessary that the Christ should suffer these things and enter into his glory?" And beginning with Moses and all the Prophets, he interpreted to them in all the Scriptures the things concerning himself." Luke 24:25-27

Forty different human authors wrote the Bible over 1,400 years. There are 66 books, 1,189 chapters, 31,102 verses, and approximately 775,000 words (depending on your translation). These are impressive statistics, as the Bible has only one message. One. The Bible, under the inspiration of the Holy Spirit, has one Author. This is why we call it the "Word of God." The underlying message and truth that this book tells us is the gospel. The "gospel" is much more than Matthew, Mark, Luke & John. The gospel, if you will, is on every page as every story points to Him.

The Old Testament is a story of how God had chosen a people, Israel, in which He would bless all the world's nations. It is through this nation that Jesus is born. The promise precedes Abraham, as it has its beginning in the beginning. It only took three chapters to see how Adam and Eve sinned in disobedience. Genesis 3:15 declares the first promise of a coming Messiah. God promised that the woman's seed would one day crush the head of the serpent, and ultimate victory over sin would be realized.

Jesus showed these two disciples what everyone else had missed on the Emmaus Road. He began with Moses (Genesis, Exodus, Leviticus, Numbers, and Deuteronomy) and went through the Prophets. What did Jesus show them? He showed them Himself. I would love to have been there as Jesus explained this to them. What a fantastic teaching to hear!

Even though that sermon was not recorded for us to hear today, we can go through the Old Testament and see Christ. The gospel reveals to me the true message of the Bible. It is none other than Jesus. Pick any book, and we will see how the story ultimately points to something greater. The Old Testament sacrificial system, law, and redemption of Israel all foreshadow the accomplishments of King Jesus. Many people like to read the Bible as a manual. The Bible is not a manual. Some read the Bible as if they were the hero of the story. I explore some of these connections in my book *The Two: Shadows of the Gospel.* I recommend you read that.

You are not the hero of the Bible. Some elevate the "heroes" of the Bible (David, Moses, Joseph, Paul, Joshua, etc.) as if the story was about them. The Bible does not contain any "heroes." Instead, the Bible tells me of one hero, one star, one main character, and it is Christ! Charles Spurgeon once said that if any thread were pulled, it would always lead to the cross. The Bible is all about the gospel. It takes the gospel to reveal this to me as I see a more remarkable story and victory within its power. How do you read the Bible? Ask yourself, every time you read, how do I see Jesus?

DISCUSSION QUESTIONS

1. How does the fact that 40 different human authors wrote the Bible over 1,400 years yet maintain one unified message impact your view of Scripture?

2. What does it mean that the Bible is the "Word of God" with one Author?

3. How does the Old Testament foreshadow and point to the coming of Jesus?

4. What are some specific examples from the Old Testament that hint at or reveal the gospel?

5. Why is it important to understand that the Bible's characters (David, Moses, Joseph, Paul, Joshua, etc.) are not the true heroes of the story? How can elevating these characters to hero status distract us from the Bible's main message?

DAY 35
THE GOSPEL REVEALS MY IDENTITY

Read: 2 Corinthians 5:17-21

"Therefore, if anyone is in Christ, he is a new creation. The old has passed away; behold, the new has come." 2 Corinthians 5:17

The question that most people ask is, "What does God want me to do?" That is a good question, but not a question we begin with. We must start with our identity to fully understand what God wants us to do. We must not start with the "doing" but with the being. You and I must ask, "Who does God say I am?" Once we know who we are, the "doing" is much more able to be known. Why is this true?

Many of us find our worth in what we do. Society values people based on what they can produce or manufacture. I am here to tell you that your worth does not come from what you do for God, but it is what God has done for you. Paul was telling the Corinthians that in Christ, we are a "new creation." This is not just a change; it's a transformation! The "old has passed away!" In Christ, we are not who we once were. In Christ, we have a new start, a fresh beginning, and a clean slate!!! If you value what you have done, you will let yourself down. All of us have failed. Our performance has let all of us down. My value has nothing to do with my accomplishments. I am valuable because God has declared me to be so in Jesus Christ.

The gospel is not our mission. It is God's mission. The gospel, the good news of Jesus Christ, is ultimately our identity. I know I stand before God in the gospel, entirely accepted, loved, and approved. I don't have to worry about my "performance" because I don't stand before him as a slave but as a son. Knowing who I am enables me to live more confidently. Why? Because Christ has already lived this life. The gospel tells me that I am "in Christ." I live in the power of His accomplishments. I can obey God because He did. I can love others because He did. I can serve God because He did. This is my new identity in Christ. The old me has passed away, and I live daily in His steps. The gospel is not just a distant truth; it's a present reality that empowers and motivates us daily.

Today, you might be struggling with your failures. If this is true, you need to awaken yourself to the reality of who God declares you to be. You do not live life alone. You live in the power of a new name, a new identity, and a past that God has forgotten. This is why it's crucial to "remind" ourselves of the gospel. This act of remembrance is not just a suggestion; it's a lifeline, a source of comfort and reassurance in times of struggle.

Paul had to "remind" the believers in the Corinthian church of the gospel (1 Corinthians 15:1-4). We need to be reminded of our new identity because we forget. We forget who we are in Christ. We suffer from gospel amnesia. What is gospel amnesia? Gospel amnesia believes the lies of the old life, such as 'I am not good enough, "I am a failure, 'or 'I am unlovable, 'and abiding in my bad news. It is forgetting who we are in Christ because of the gospel. Gospel amnesia understands the gospel only as a ticket to another place and not as identification for life. The gospel is for believers!

The gospel reveals my real identity and worth before God. I have value, not because of my obedience but because of Jesus' obedience. Grow in grace and the knowledge of the gospel. Wake up from your gospel amnesia and stop believing the lies we are so prone to believe. The gospel light gloriously proclaims that we are IN CHRIST!

DISCUSSSION QUESTIONS

1. How does knowing who we are in Christ help us understand what God wants us to do?

2. How does society often measure a person's worth, and how does this differ from the way God measures our worth? Why is it important to base our value on what God has done for us rather than our own accomplishments?

3. What does it mean to be a "new creation" in Christ according to 2 Corinthians 5:17? How does the concept of the "old passing away" and the "new coming" apply to your personal life?

☐

WEEK 6

THE LIGHT OF OUR PRAISE

DAY 36
PRAISE THE LORD

"Praise the Lord! Praise God in his sanctuary; praise him in his mighty heavens!" - Psalm 150:1

We delight in celebrating, don't we? We are a people who revel in joyous gatherings and feasts. Birthdays, anniversaries, holidays, promotions, memories, and accomplishments are the milestones that bring us together and fill our hearts with joy. This desire to celebrate, I believe, is a gift from our Creator. God has instilled in His people a natural inclination to praise. He bestowed upon Israel numerous feasts and occasions to remember. Not only are we naturally inclined to praise, but we are also commanded to do so.

Praise the Lord! These three words carry profound meaning. The Hebrew word for 'praise' signifies 'boasting' or 'to make much of.' In the context of this study, it also conveys the idea of "shining."Therefore, when we praise God, we 'shine'. The essence of praise is to magnify and celebrate God. How do we accomplish this? Psalm 150 provides us with a guide on 'how to 'Praise the Lord! First, the object of our praise is the LORD. Notice that this is in all capital letters. Whenever you see the name

"LORD," it is because the official name of God is used. Transliterated into English, this name makes four letters YHWH. You may have heard Yahweh refer to God. This is the closest we can understand how to pronounce these four unpronounceable Hebrew consonants. God is worthy of all of our praise.

Secondly, we are told to "praise" GOD in His sanctuary and "mighty heavens." The sanctuary is most likely a reference to where God dwells. God lives in a Holy Place that is much different from our fallen environment. Heaven is breathtaking, and no words could ever do it justice. The "mighty heavens" refers not to where God dwells but to the sky and the universe. Looking up at the sky and seeing the vast expanse of the universe is humbling. We are so small in comparison, yet God created each star and has a name for each one. God created all of this for His glory, and He is to be praised.

So often, our praise of God is limited by our small or stripped-down version of Him. Many fail to see the bigness of God because other things or people become bigger to them. How much more should we "Praise the Lord?" If I were to understand His "sanctuary" and the vastness of His "mighty heavens," it might begin to help. How high is your view and praise of God? What else is stealing the praise and light in your life from Him? It's crucial to understand the bigness of God to truly appreciate His glory and praise Him accordingly.

Praise the Lord!

DISCUSSION QUESTIONS

1. What does the Hebrew word for 'praise' signify, and how does it relate to our worship of God? In what ways can we "shine" when we praise God?

2. Why is it important to understand that the object of our praise is the LORD (YHWH)?

3. How does having a small or stripped-down view of God limit our praise of Him?

DAY 37
EXCELLENT GREATNESS

Praise him for his mighty deeds; praise him according to his excellent greatness! Psalm 150:2

Many have a fascination with sports athletes, don't we? Many worship, magnify, and celebrate their abilities and achievements. We speak of their greatness based on statistics and championships. We remember their names long after death and cherish their accomplishments while they live. We retire their numbers, write books about them, and sometimes even make movies about their lives. They give us a sense of achievement, which inspires us to accomplish goals and reach beyond our dreams. At times, we may even live our lives through them. We know we may never be that famous or successful, so their accomplishments become ours. Which is probably why we use the word "we" when our teams wins the game. "We won the game!" "We are the champions!"

Michael Jordan is the best basketball player to have ever stepped on a basketball court. As a die-hard New York Knicks fan, I loathed his "Air-ness." He was the reason that kept my Knicks from winning a championship during their best years. He gave me stomach cramps and many unhappy nights, as the Knicks could never find a way to stop him. After winning his third championship, he shocked the sports world by retiring from basketball to pursue a professional baseball career. That didn't pan out too well for him. He eventually came back to basketball and won three more championships. He is celebrated today as the best player to have ever played. It's easy for people to praise Michael Jordan because they have seen what Michael Jordan has done.

What have you seen God do? What has God done for you? The Psalmist writes that we are to "praise Him for His mighty deeds." How often do you reflect and celebrate what God has done? His deeds, far surpassing those of a basketball player, are unique and awe-inspiring. I encourage you in your prayer time to begin every prayer with a recount of praise. Thank God for creating, saving, and providing for you! Take a moment and take in a gorgeous sunset. Step out for a few minutes after dark and observe the countless stars in the sky. Take a moment and look at your spouse and thank God for them! When my kids were very young, I would go into their rooms and watch them sleep. Watching their chests rise and fall with every breath brought tears to my eyes. God has been so kind and gracious to me. I don't deserve any of this. Thank you, God!

We are to also praise Him "according to His excellent greatness." We all know God is great, but did you know He is excellently great? His greatness is not a one-time event, but a continuous state of being. The light of our praise comes from a gospel-renewed and gospel-transformed heart. Our God is worthy of our praise and much more than we can even give. He is so great that heaven never stops praising, nor should we. This continuous greatness should inspire us to praise Him without ceasing.

"And the four living creatures, each of them with six wings, are full of eyes all around and within, and day and night they never cease to say, "Holy, holy, holy, is the Lord God Almighty, Who was and is and is to come!" And whenever the living creatures give glory and honor and thanks to Him who is seated on the throne, Who lives forever and ever, the twenty-four elders fall down before Him who is seated on the throne and worship Him who lives forever and ever. They cast their crowns before the throne, saying, "Worthy are You, our Lord and God, to receive glory and honor and power, for You created all things, and by Your will they existed and were created." Revelation 4: 8-11

DISCUSSION QUESTIONS

1. What are some of the mighty deeds God has done that you have seen in your life?

2. How often do you take the time to reflect on and celebrate what God has done for you?

3. How can beginning your prayer with praise and recounting God's deeds change your perspective?

4. What are some specific deeds of God that you can praise Him for today?

5. What does it mean to you that God is "excellently great"? How can recognizing God's continuous greatness inspire you to praise Him more consistently?

DAY 38
MADE TO WORSHIP

Praise him with trumpet sound; praise him with lute and harp!
Praise him with tambourine and dance; praise him with strings
and pipe! Praise him with sounding cymbals; praise him with
loud clashing cymbals! Let everything that has breath praise the
Lord! Praise the Lord! - Psalm 150:3-6

Why are we here? Are we just one giant cosmic accident? No. We were created for God and to enjoy Him forever. We were made to worship our Creator and for Him to be our greatest desire and joy. The Psalmist concludes this short but powerful Psalm by announcing the responsibility of everything that has "breath" to praise! This breath that was breathed into Adam made him a living being. Our parents have passed down this breath ever since Adam and Eve. The breath of life that God has given is to be returned to Him in praise. I love how the Psalmist includes the different ways to praise God. These ways include tambourines, dance, strings, pipes, and cymbals; it all resounds in the praise of God. The notes and sounds of the instruments delight the same God who created sound itself. Let us lift our voices and worship this God who created music for the express purpose of worship, and in doing so, find true joy and transformation.

When we give the praise due to God to anything else, we are guilty of idolatry. Similarly, when we live contrary to the life God has called us to live, we are also guilty of idolatry. However, God created each of us with a unique purpose, and it is in aligning our lives with this purpose that we find true joy. This joy is not fleeting but deep and lasting, surpassing all understanding. It is a joy that inspires and gives hope. Why does He deserve my praise? The answer to this question could only be partially exhausted.

There is not enough paper to fully express God's worth. We could only begin to skim the surface as we dwell on His praiseworthiness. However, once the praise of this God begins, it will forever change you! This God is to be praised in all that He does and for all who He is. He is unique, with no equal. There is no comparable foe that could stand against Him. He alone is worthy to be praised. It is why the universe shouts when men don't. It is why the birds sing when men can't. His name and glory are the very reason why everything exists! You were made to worship.

DISCUSSION QUESTIONS

1. Why do you think the question "Why are we here?" is so significant for people to answer?

2. How does the idea that we were created for God and to enjoy Him forever change your perspective on life?

3. How does worshiping God bring true joy and transformation in our lives?

4. Share a time when you experienced deep joy through worship?

5. The Psalmist mentions that the universe and birds praise God even when humans don't. What does this teach us about creation's role in worship? How can observing nature lead us to a greater appreciation and praise of God?

DAY 39
THE PRAISE OF THANKSGIVING

Therefore, as you received Christ Jesus the Lord, so walk in him, rooted and built up in him and established in the faith, just as you were taught, abounding in thanksgiving. Colossians 2:6-7

I love Thanksgiving. It is one of my favorite holidays. What is there not to love about it? Thanksgiving gives the excitement of food, friends, family, and football. Yes, more, please! It is essential because at the heart of praise is thankfulness. Being thankful is an overflow of the gospel infiltrating every nook and cranny of our hearts. Paul tells us in Colossians 2 that our lives are to be "rooted and built up" in Christ. This is the key to being thankful.

The fuel for thankfulness is a heart that is rooted in Christ. How does this happen? It begins with a proper understanding of God's grace. When you pause and realize God's greatness, thankfulness should be your heart's response. Once we understand how God has blessed us, the grace of God becomes much more evident in our lives. Being thankful is not just about the good things or times of life. It's about cultivating a heart of gratitude through regular spiritual practices, such as prayer, meditation, and reading the Bible. These practices help us to stay rooted in Christ and to see His grace in every aspect of our lives.

"Give thanks in all circumstances; for this is the will of God in Christ Jesus for you." - I Thessalonians 5:18 It is much easier to praise God for things that bring us peace and comfort. But the true test of our faith and gratitude is when we can be thankful even in the midst of trials. Being thankful through trials is not easy, but it is an overflow of the gospel in our hearts. Have you ever had a peace you could not describe during a time that did not make sense? This is the power of thankfulness in all circumstances.

If we say that God is good during the good times, we must also believe He is good during the bad times. God doesn't change even though our circumstances do. When we are thankful, we are allowing the light of praise to shine from our hearts. This light shows the goodness of God. Thankfulness is a heart issue. If you are not thankful, take the time to check your heart. How are you being rooted and built in Christ? Do you read the Bible regularly? Are you around other believers who can help you grow and pray for you? I encourage you to take a moment to reflect on your own gratitude and how you can cultivate a more thankful heart.

We are by nature an unthankful people. We whine, complain, and have bad attitudes when life doesn't appear to have gone our way. To complain and gripe is to tell the world that God has ceased being good. You may not admit that out loud, but you convey that belief when you stop being thankful. To have a complaining spirit is to tell God that you deserve better. Having this complaining spirit completely misses the point of grace. Grace is receiving from God what I do not deserve. What do you deserve? Do you want God to treat you the way He should? The answer to that question is not. God is not fair, so you should be extremely thankful. Overflowing thankfulness is contagious! Who are you influencing with your spirit of thankfulness? Put your life in perspective. But remember, your joy should come from God's presence, not your circumstances. This is the source of true, unshakeable joy.

DISCUSSION QUESTIONS

1. How does being thankful relate to the gospel infiltrating every part of our hearts?

2. What does it mean to have our lives "rooted and built up" in Christ, and how does this foster thankfulness?

3. Discuss 1 Thessalonians 5:18 and its call to give thanks in all circumstances. What does this mean to you?

4. Have you ever experienced a peace that didn't make sense during a difficult time? Share your experience.

DAY 40
THE PRAISE OF HIS GLORIOUS GRACE

"So for the second time they called the man who had been blind and said to him, "Give glory to God. We know that this man is a sinner." He answered, "Whether he is a sinner I do not know. One thing I do know, that though I was blind, now I see." - John 9:24-25

Heaven is going to be an amazing place. The Bible declares its beauty is too much for human words to describe fully. We will see our friends and family who have gone before us into eternity. However, the part I am most looking forward to is the stories. Heaven will be filled with the stories of redeemed people who were radically and gloriously saved. These people, from all walks of life, will bring a rich tapestry of experiences, personalities, and ethnicities. There will be those whom God saved from a life of debauchery and others who were saved from a seemingly "moral" life. No matter how each story unfolds, one thing will be unmistakably clear. Every story will include undeserving and lost sinners who were chosen (Ephesians 1:4), loved (Ephesians 1:4, 5), redeemed, and forgiven (Ephesians 1:7). These are the stories that I want to hear. These are the stories that will never grow old. Every story will be told to the "praise of His glorious grace" (Ephesians 1:6). Heaven will not be dull.

In John 9, we read the story of a blind man that Jesus healed. The change in the man made a radical difference. People who wanted to arrest Jesus and charge Him with blasphemy approached this blind man. He had a story that needed to be told. How is a man who was born from birth now able to see? How is this radical life change possible? The testimony of the people who knew him while he was blind was enough proof that he wasn't lying. What did this man do? What kind of evangelism program did he use? What kind of techniques did he learn? None. The man did all that he knew to do. He said exactly what happened to him. He said, "I was blind, now I see."

Every day of your life is another chapter of the story of God's grace. We all have something to share as we celebrate what God has done, is doing, and will do. Your personal experiences, no matter how big or small, are important and can inspire others. Don't hesitate to share them; we are all here to support and encourage each other.

I pray that you have been changed during these last 40 days. I pray that you have been broken over sin, challenged to read God's Word, burdened over lost people, called to love the church, impacted by the

Gospel, and left with a spirit of thankful, unending praise.

DISCUSSION QUESTIONS

1. Why are stories of radical and glorious salvation so compelling?

2. According to Ephesians 1:4-7, what are the key elements of the redemption story for every believer?

3. How does recognizing each day as a chapter in the story of God's grace change your perspective on daily life?

4. What are some ways you can celebrate and acknowledge what God is doing in your life right now?

5. In what ways have you been changed over the past 40 days?

Made in the USA
Middletown, DE
14 July 2024

57260457R00106